"This is a book of monumental importance ~~~ or Gen-Zer looking to kick-off their career or take it to the next level. Mark's tough-love approach gives insight into how to be successful—working for it! A must read for anyone looking for direct career coaching and honest advice on professional introspection."

STEPHANIE CUTTER, co-founder of and partner at Precision, former co-host of CNN's *Crossfire*, and former Deputy Campaign Manager for Barack Obama

———

"Navigating the job market and then distinguishing yourself once you're in the door has never been more difficult. *The #PACE Process for Early Career Success* is the playbook that every emerging talent needs. This book answers the questions on everyone's minds and does so through an insider's lens. If you choose to read this book, know that you are at an immediate advantage against those that have not read it. Buy, read, and follow the guidance in *The #PACE Process*. Doing so will be the first, best decision of your long career ahead."

MIKE GLASS, Vice President Global Talent
Thermo Fisher Scientific

———

"Whether you are looking for your first job or already starting to climb the corporate ladder, *The #PACE Process for Early Career Success* is an invaluable resource for moving the needle quickly on your rise up the career ladder. The book is an easy read with tangible insights, strategies, and tactics giving you an edge in the career marketplace and enabling you to hit your career goals and aspirations. A must-read for any young professional."

ALAN OSETEK, Global Digital, and Adtech Executive

————

"If you are starting out in your career and looking for outstanding practical guidance on achieving career success, then you must read this book. You will learn how to build your network, differentiate yourself, build your personal brand and attain your desired opportunities. Zides builds on years of experience to provide those just starting out a roadmap for career success."

BRAD JOHNSON, Babson College Lecturer and former
Vice President, Wayfair

————

"I've known Mark Zides for over 20 years both personally and professionally, and can attest firsthand Mark has not only developed, but has embodied *The #PACE Process for Early Career Success* his entire adult life. Take a lesson from "Coach Z" in this easy-to-follow guide towards early career success. Simple but not simplistic, it's an invaluable resource to prepare and kickstart your career through proven real life examples and experiences from the author himself."

JIM COGHLIN, Vice Chairman & Chief Supply Chain Officer,
Coghlin Companies

————

"Have had the pleasure of knowing Mark Zides since our college days and have watched him continue to always put himself in a position to be successful. He lives his life the way he articulates #PACE—with #PACE! Having the tools and techniques to advocate for your best career trajectory is a must in today's world. *The #PACE Process* is a mandatory read for any person who strives to find success in any career situation."

JOHN LENTINE, PTC, DVP Sales – Americas

———

"In the 30 years of knowing Mark, I have had the opportunity to watch him pursue his passion of helping younger generations grow in their careers. He has brought his widely known motto, #PACE to life in *The #PACE Process to Career Success* and it couldn't be more spot on. He uses easy to understand, actionable topics that drive home what the corporate world is expecting of you. Mark nails it in his approach to helping younger generations acclimate and succeed in the professional realm, and I can't imagine not having my children read this when at a crossroads in their careers."

WOODY HINES, Executive Vice President,
Emerging Medical Technologies Ventures

———

"This book provides practical strategies for this new generation to be successful in their pursuit of the dream job or destination company. Perfect for young professionals competing in today's marketplace!"

CURTIS JONES, Global Learning Leader,
International Global Financial Services Firm

THE #PACE

Library of Congress Control Number: 2022930540

ISBN (paperback):978-1-956450-16-3
       (eBook): 978-1-956450-17-0

 Armin Lear Press Inc
215 W Riverside Drive, #4362
Estes Park, CO 80517

THE#PACE

Process for Early
Career Success

Mark Zides

For my wife, Rachel. Thank you for supporting me through our journey together.

For my family and all those who supported me and helped me write this book. Thank you for helping me keep the #PACE.

And for my kids, this book was written for you.

CONTENTS

FOREWORD

WHEN MARK ZIDES, my friend of more than two decades, told me he was writing a book, I assumed he was talking about a memoir. I've known Mark since 1995, when I first became his CFO, CPA, and financial advisor. We've been friends ever since. I've golfed with him, gone to Patriots games with him, and had plenty of frank conversations with him about the nature of success and what it takes to achieve your goals.

Mark's journey to becoming CEO of Coreaxis spanned multiple companies and financial crashes, with plenty of speed bumps and false starts. He's had to redefine himself more than once, rebuilding from nothing to make his vision for his work and life a reality. I'll never lose my admiration for the way he was able to bounce back from every roadblock he faced to establish and grow one of the most influential corporate training consultancies in the world. The story of his path to success could be a book in its own right.

You can imagine my surprise, then, when Mark replied, "I'm not writing a memoir. I'm writing a career success guidebook for recent graduates and early career professionals." The more Mark told me about his reasons for writing The #Pace Process for Early Career Success, the more I came to love the concept. He explained how he became interested in the ways young adults navigate the early stages of their careers, and how he grew increasingly troubled by the patterns he encountered. These were patterns I have also observed in my own work, but had never been able to put into words. As Mark put it, most young workers have simply never been given the tools for succeeding in the workplace, and it's evident in the way they plan and execute on a daily basis. With remote work on the rise, the way we think about what makes a successful career is changing rapidly. We're living in the age of the Great Resignation, which sees young workers leaving their jobs en masse in search of something better.

But what does "better" look like? How will you know it when you see it? Most importantly, once you know what you want, how can you achieve it?

Mark Zides has been there, and his success speaks for itself. He's put in the work, identified the keys to achieving bigger and better, and used them to win in his own career journey. Now, he's sharing those techniques with the next generation—a generation that's facing unprecedented changes and challenges in the post-COVID landscape. A few key skills will be critical for launching a career in the digital age, and they aren't the hard skills! Most talent experts agree that what matters most for long-term job success isn't knowing Python, speaking fluent French, or having a certificate in data analysis. Those are important tools for some jobs, but, the ability to lead, communicate, adapt to change, and problem-solve when things don't go your way, (without taking it personally) are the most important skills that young professionals need to obtain for their long term success.

Mark's #Pace philosophy addresses these issues for young workers that are relatively new to the workforce. We're not talking about checking off a list of requirements or going through the motions to get what you want. We're talking about developing a learning mindset, a nose for opportunity, the desire to go after what you want without settling for "good enough", and, above all, the ability to handle setbacks without losing your head. To #Pace yourself is to know what you want, keep your goals at the front of your mind, and be willing to do what you need to achieve your desired level of success.

Mark isn't just a dreamer; he's a doer. He knows from firsthand experience what it takes to get your career off the ground, and he isn't afraid to call you out on the behaviors and mindsets that are holding you back. From networking to landing that first job to climbing the ladder in a remote workplace, he has created a roadmap to success that goes beyond statistics and to-do lists that will help you unpack your mental blocks and overcome obstacles. This guide will teach you to do more than just aspire; it will teach you to achieve. This is The #Pace Process for Early Career Success.

— JOE LAZAREK
Partner
Morris & Morris

THE #PACE PROCESS

DISTILLING A LIFETIME'S WORTH of information into something that's not just useful, but also digestible, is no easy task. As I sat down to write this, a lot of questions came up for me: *Is this worth passing on? Will it help others the same way it helped me? What's universal, and what's unique to my story or situation?* There's no one-size-fits-all approach to finding success. Different industries function in different ways, emphasize different skills, and move at different rates. What works for a lawyer might not work for a doctor, a writer, or a banker. That's the challenge with writing a general career guide: *How do you possibly account for everyone's individual situation?*

There are lots of practical methods of navigating your career, but when I sat down and looked back on my own experience, and on what parts of it I most wanted other people to internalize, the practical stuff wasn't what stood out as the most impactful. What really stuck with me, and what kept me going over the years even as I changed roles and industries, was the mental stuff—call it perspective, call it mindset, call it a lifestyle. So while I cover all those practical aspects in this book, the #Pace Process is more about incorporating the right mindset into each of those practical steps.

The concept of *#Pace* is something I return to throughout this book. It is a term I coined years ago, and it's since become a motto. My team and I will shoot it back and forth, saying things like, "Remember #Pace," or adding *#Pace* to our emails and communications. When you have #Pace, you're striving to be the best at what you do, and then realizing your goals. You're #Pace-ing yourself—going for a level of performance that's high, but also *sustainable*. My hope is that by the time you finish this book, you'll be better equipped to find your own #Pace—the right one for your career and personal goals. It's not about keeping pace with *others*, it is about finding and staying true to *your own #Pace.*

As you read this, I want you to always have #Pace in the back of your mind. When you think about applying the suggestions I give you here, always do so in service to the question, *"How can I use this to succeed?"* Remember, this guide is just as much about getting into the right frame of mind as it is about doing the practical stuff. I'm a firm believer that perspective is a huge predictor for success. Your actions are a direct reflection of your mindset. If you half-ass it, you won't get anywhere. If your heart's not in it, you'll never shine. You have to want it and live it—from when you wake up in the morning to when you go to bed at night. If you can do that, you're already halfway there.

> *"The Way To Get Started Is To Quit Talking*
> *And Begin Doing."*
> —Walt Disney

INTRODUCTION

EXPERTS PREDICT THAT BY 2025, employees under the age of forty will make up the majority of the world's workforce.[1] Odds are, if you're reading this book, you're one of the millions of young adults making the transition into full-time work or are in the early stages of your career and looking for ways to grow. That transition isn't easy, and in today's digital, globalized world, it's more intimidating than ever.

Not only do you have to survive in a larger, more connected world, but the very structure of work has changed. Office jobs have evolved into remote jobs and hybrid jobs. The post-COVID-19 workspace has changed how we work. "In a recent report out of Accenture, 83 percent of 9,326 workers surveyed say they prefer a hybrid model—in which they can work remotely at least 25 percent of the time."[2] Likely, you are part of this group and that will change the types of jobs you are looking for as well as how you will go about applying for them.

Are you ready for it? Do you know what you want to do for a living? Where do you see yourself in three, five, or ten years? If people haven't started asking you these questions, they soon will, and you'll be expected to know the answers—so start by asking yourself the less obvious of these questions.

- How do you measure your success?
- How will you get there?
- What stands between where you are and where you want to be?

WHO AM I, AND WHY SHOULD YOU CARE?

That's always such a loaded question, isn't it? You probably want to know why I'm qualified to be giving career advice in the first place, so I'll start with this: I'm the founder and CEO of CoreAxis, a company that provides employee training and talent solutions for companies such as Amazon, ThermoFisher Scientific, Netflix, Nestle, and more. I founded CoreAxis twenty years ago with the mission to help, educate, and mentor people.

There's a lot to my story, but the most important thing you need to know is that I was born into a working-class family. We were not wealthy by any means. I was brought up in Massachusetts by two working parents—my mom was a phlebotomist, and my dad was a truck driver—and that experience taught me entrepreneurship and all the core values that I have lived by. I've been hustling all my life, from shoveling driveways as a kid to selling my 401k to fund my first company (which I founded from my basement).

The second most important thing you need to know about me is that my own career path hasn't been straightforward or smooth sailing. I graduated from Babson College with a degree in Finance Investments, thinking I wanted to work on Wall Street, before pivoting into software training. The first company I founded, Progressive Solutions, was on the verge of going public before the market crashed in 2000, and I had to change gears again, doing freelance consulting work all while starting CoreAxis. I went from job to job until finally deciding to take the plunge and go all-in on CoreAxis at the end of 2008. The United States was in the middle of the Great Recession, and it was the worst time to start a business. I ended up selling my 401k a second time to keep the lights on, but we survived the recession and have been growing ever since.

All this is to say, I know what it's like to coast in your career, especially in your twenties and thirties. I had plenty of false starts and dead ends during my journey, but by learning to properly prepare, focus on my path, take risks, and not let failure get me down, I made it past all the speedbumps. My mentality was that I needed to roll up my sleeves, work hard, and get the job done, no matter the risk. It's not easy and is often scary. Anyone who says differently is lying. But through work, dedication, and tenacity, I kickstarted my career and found success—and so can you.

WHO THIS BOOK IS FOR

This is going to sound strange, especially since I've just gone on about my life as an entrepreneur, but this book isn't meant (exclusively) for entrepreneurs. I want to give a holistic look at the job-hunting process, from networking to interviewing to promotions, as well as a comprehensive approach to finding success in your career once you get the job. This means that some sections will be more applicable to your specific situation than others. However, the soft skills and general techniques I describe here are applicable to anyone, from startup founders to freelancers to people in more traditional corporate jobs. This book is for you if you need direction, no matter where you are on your path. Think of it as a pocket career coach. Maybe you're just out of college and you're not sure where to start. Maybe you've been working for a while and feel like you've hit a dead-end. Perhaps you're returning to the workforce after time away to raise your kids or after military service. Whatever your situation, this guide will help you navigate this new world of work—be it hybrid, remote, or other—and find the level of success you desire.

That said, I can't make it happen for you. You have to take ownership of your career, your choices, and your #Pace. No one else can or will do it for you. I'm here to give you tools to do this, but tools are only as good as the person using them. You have to want it and you have to be willing to put in the work to apply these guidelines to your life. Anyone can read a self-help book, but if you aren't willing to make an effort to use the advice I give you, you'll end up frustrated and unsuccessful. Success comes from hard work, dedication to your career vision, and a commitment to your own personal growth. Own that mindset starting now.

WHAT TO EXPECT AS YOU READ

I'm known for being direct and easy-to-read. I'm easy-going in my work, but I also don't beat around the bush, which is why some of the things I discuss in this book might rub you the wrong way. Some of it might come across as harsh, but that's because I believe that sugar-coating things is doing you a disservice. If you have a problem that's getting in the way of your success, would you want your career coach to tell you it's all hunky-dory and never give you a chance to address it? Or would you want them to tell you firmly that what you're doing isn't working and offer you some suggestions to fix it?

I'm invested in your success. If what I say resonates with you, great! But if not, I would ask you to keep an open mind, even if what I say ruffles your feathers. I'm speaking from personal experience when I say that accepting feedback, even when it's negative, is the biggest favor you can do for yourself. More on that later.

At the end of each chapter, I include a list of #PACE Process Steps that you can use in different areas of your career. These are the most essential points from each section, and the advice that I believe is most crucial.

Remember, your career is your future. By investing in it now, you're setting yourself up for a lifetime of success.

SECTION 1

PREPARE

#PACE: **PREPARE** + APPLY + COMMIT + EXPLORE

TODAY'S COMPETITIVE JOB LANDSCAPE has boulders, wild-fires, and quicksand. If you don't believe me when I say it is hard to launch and advance a career, here are some hard-hitting truths about the reality of job-hunting in the twenty-first century as a recent college graduate:

- A study conducted in 2017 revealed that:
  - » 54 percent of recent graduates self-reported as underemployed.[3]
  - » 45 percent of recent graduates found it "difficult or extremely difficult" to find a job.[4]

Things look equally bleak from the perspective of the guys doing the hiring. For example:

- Businesses are reporting a growing lack of qualified candidates among college graduates.[5,6]

- A 2021 survey revealed that employers are most concerned with incoming candidates' lack of ability to "manage [their] career, [their] boss, and those around [them]." In other words, career savvy.[7]

Why, though? What's so different about this generation that's made it so hard to get your foot in the door? There are a few reasons and some of them might surprise you. Others might not. Either way, I believe the only way to solve a problem is to figure out why it exists in the first place.

- With the rise of the gig economy, more and more traditional jobs are going to freelancers and independent contractors.[8]
- On average, 300,000 jobs are sent overseas every year, costing millions of Americans their employment. This number is on the rise.[9,10]
- Outsourcing isn't just for "unskilled labor." More and more jobs, from IT and quality assurance, to accounting and even *law,* are being outsourced, whether to different cities or different countries.[11,12]
- Recruitment automation means that 75 percent of résumés are rejected before they're even seen by a human.[13]
- 70 percent of currently-employed participants in a recent TopResume survey claimed to be keeping their eyes peeled for new job opportunities.[14]

As someone who's presumably trying to kickstart your career, what does this mean for you? It means the race to employment is on—and that race can seem never-ending at times. It doesn't matter where you're looking; gone are the days of easy job-hunting. The internet has opened up the playing field to virtually everyone else on the planet. Getting hired is a project in and of itself and moving up the work ladder is even more difficult than that. Add that to the effects of COVID-19 on the economy and job market, and the move into a remote and/or hybrid workplace, and it's easy to get discouraged.

THE GOOD NEWS: THERE IS HOPE.

I promised you earlier that I wasn't going to sugarcoat things for you, and I meant it. I'm not going to coddle you, and I'm not going to tell you that the universe works in mysterious ways. I'm going to tell you that you need to work for everything that you have. The truth is that success is harder to come by these days than it used to be. It's not fair, I know. But life's not fair. Complaining about it isn't going to change anything.

You *can* and *will* find success in your career, despite the current obstacles, and making it happen is surprisingly simple. Not necessarily *easy*—as they say, "If it were easy, everyone would do it," but it is completely doable. All you need to do is take a risk and invest in yourself. Take the risk, dive in headfirst, and don't look back.

On average, every corporate job opening attracts two hundred and fifty applicants. Typically, around six of them are given interviews, one to three make it to the final round, and only one is hired.[15,16] Among those applicants, there will be many who are just like you: young, talented, and intelligent.

What will set you apart and what I hope to impart to you are the things that aren't taught in school: Grit. Determination. Savviness. Effective networking. A nose for opportunity. An understanding of your niche and how to leverage it to get what you want. A drive toward success. You'll have to work harder than earlier generations, harder than you've probably ever worked in your life.

Ultimately, you are solely responsible for winning the game of career success, but you can't win any game without the right strategy. Vince Lombardi said it best: "The harder you work, the harder it is to surrender."

CHAPTER 1

START WITH THE RIGHT MINDSET

BRACE YOURSELF: THERE'S MORE TOUGH LOVE ON THE WAY.
It's human nature not to want to recognize our flaws. Hell, I'm as guilty of it as anyone. But the problem is that other people will see them, even if you don't. And sometimes these people, whether they be employers, clients, or investors, will form a view of you without you realizing it. And they are people who have the power to influence the direction of your career. If you don't confront your flaws head on, and without becoming defensive, you just won't climb to the heights you could otherwise.

I believe that anyone can learn to build grit and strengthen themselves against the challenges of the world. Anyone can improve their ability to take things in stride instead of allowing bad news and conflict to offend them or knock them down. These are the skills you will need in order to find success in the workplace, and in order to harness these skills, you need to learn to silence that inner sensitivity, adopt a mindset that is open to feedback—both positive and critical—and constantly strive to do better. Not for anyone else, but for yourself.

SPECIAL ISN'T WHAT IT'S CRACKED UP TO BE

In 1996, Chuck Palahniuk wrote the novel *Fight Club*, which was turned into the smash-hit film of the same name in 1999. At one point in the book, main character Tyler Durden berates a group of his followers, telling them, "You are not special. You are not a beautiful and unique snowflake. You're the same decaying organic matter as everything else."[17] This is believed to be the origin of the expression of being a snowflake, however it did not enter the mainstream until the late 2010s, when commentators began using it to refer to entitled, overly-sensitive people. Snowflakes are afraid of ideas they disagree with. They've lost the ability to engage in thoughtful debate and discourse. They are easily offended, wearing blinders toward any views outside their own. So why am I bringing this up now? Because regardless of how anyone feels about the term itself, the issue of being overly-sensitive is pertinent to career success—and really success of any kind.

Yes, this term is overly politicized, and far too broadly applied. It's also not a definition that applies to everyone. There are overly-sensitive, entitled people of all ages—it's not exclusive to any one generation. You might be the toughest, most tenacious, hardest working person in the world. Maybe you've had a lifetime of character building and are just looking for a way to harness it. The term snowflake may not apply to you an any way, shape, or form. But as with most expressions, there is a grain of truth to it; such people do exist. Even if you aren't one yourself, you'll likely have to work for or with one at some point in your career. And that's what we are going to confront, head on, in this chapter. We can't shy away from the hard things in life.

Palahniuk later wrote an essay for *Entertainment Weekly* elaborating what he meant, and his explanation has a familiar ring to it. Discussing his own experience as a young adult, Palahniuk wrote, "Everyone [was] saying, 'you're wonderful just the way you are. You're perfect.' ... A lifetime of disingenuous, one-size-fits-all praise had kept most of my peers from pushing hard to achieve any actual triumphs."[18]

I think this is a great explanation of the first part of being a snowflake: this idea of being perfect just as you are, with no need to examine yourself or try to change and *grow*. This is what happens when people—people who have grown up being told that they are the center of the universe and that the world must bend to their every whim and feeling—come of age. The result is an overwhelming sense of entitlement and fragility that's out-of-touch with the (sometimes uncomfortable) realities of the work world. And again, this is not unique to any one generation. There are examples throughout history, however I do worry that the incident rate is increasing. That's a trend I want to help change.

I'm not trying to say that sensitivity and security are inherently bad. The problem is when they go too far. When people learn to expect the world to walk on eggshells for them instead of expecting it to challenge them, they don't know how to deal with those challenges when they do come... and come they will. Try to imagine what this mentality will do to you in a work environment, where you're surrounded by difficult tasks, strict deadlines, and coworkers who aren't there to cater to your every whim.

HOW DOES THIS AFFECT YOU?

As people enter the workforce, they need to learn how to successfully navigate issues like rejection, loss, competition, regret, fatigue, burnout, and difficult clients without getting discouraged, and that means building grit, stamina, and perseverance. Waiting for your work environment to adjust to your desires and expectations perfectly is not an option. Especially in the new realities of the hybrid work-place. Yes, there will be more flexibility. But you will have to make compromises in other ways. Waiting for something perfect to come along will inevitably lead to disappointment, and then to frustration. You may come to resent not just your job, but your entire career, or even the idea of work in general. The truth is that we live in an imperfect world, and you need to learn how to buckle down and persevere, even when things don't go your way.

There *is* a time and a place for demanding change, and we will discuss that more in later chapters, but you will have to learn to pick your battles. Allowing differing viewpoints and perceived offenses to rule your life will only wear you down. It will make others less likely to see you as worth their time, attention, and respect. And it will set you up for failure in the face of real adversity. There's a balance to be found (and we will address that in Section 3) and taking care of your mental health is very important, but starting your career with a put-upon, persecuted mindset is not the way to do it. This may require rethinking your own day-to-day habits and thought patterns, and sincerely trying to understand others' perspectives. It will mean putting in the effort without the guarantee of instant gratification. It won't be easy, but it will put you firmly on the path to success.

#PACE PROCESS STEPS

- **Don't take things personally.** Especially when they aren't directed at you. Work on shaking things off and letting others handle their own battles. Remember, words only hold as much value as you give them. Eleanor Roosevelt really put it best: "No one can make you feel inferior without your consent."

- **Don't expect the world to cater to you.** No work environment is perfect. There will be plenty of minor inconveniences, especially when it comes to your first job. Wait and watch for the right time to make suggestions and voice ideas about your role, your workplace, and your coworkers.

- **Pick your battles and fight them yourself.** Throughout your life, you will experience conflict. You won't get along perfectly with everyone, but you'll have to figure out if a problem is worth addressing. If the problem *is* worth addressing, see if you can handle it yourself before escalating up the chain of command. Managers will want to be involved in these issues eventually, but they will respect you more if you show you tried to handle it yourself first.

- **Look for context.** It will save you a lot of hand wringing and free you up to focus on what's important. If your manager snapped at you, was it because they hated your guts or because they were having a bad day? If your team shot down your suggestion, was it because they were out to get you or because the problem needed a different solution? Assume the best of people—until they prove otherwise.

- **You aren't always right.** Open your mind to the possibility that other people know more than you and are better at some things than you. It is okay to be wrong. It's pretty common advice now to "surround yourself with people smarter than you." It's because it is an opportunity to *learn*.

CHAPTER 2

BOOTSTRAPPING 101

THERE'S THIS MISCONCEPTION that job hunting is an in-and-out, open-and-shut kind of thing: you send your résumé off to a few places, making a couple of tweaks to your cover letter along the way, and then just sit on your couch twiddling your thumbs until the offers start rolling in.

Wouldn't that be nice?

The truth is, getting your foot in the door is a task in and of itself. It takes effort, focus, and persistence. (Are you sensing a theme here?) I'm sure by now you've heard the phrase, "picking yourself up by your bootstraps." If you strip away all the political connotations, there's still something interesting underneath. It's true that no one succeeds in this world without a little help. After all, success doesn't happen in a vacuum. Bootstrapping, contrary to popular belief these days, isn't snapping your fingers and magically opening doors. Instead, it's about forming connections from the ground up, leveraging them, and using your situation, background, and unique assets—whatever they are—in a strategic way to make that first step onto the ladder. And then doing the same thing over and over again for each successive step on that ladder.

Something to note here is that the hybrid workplace will make this more difficult. Without being physically in the office with your colleagues and managers, you will lose out on some of the interactions and bonding that are more common in the traditional office setting. So you will have to get more creative in this brand new world. More on that later.

HUSTLING IS A LIFESTYLE

According to writer Malcolm Gladwell, citing expertise expert Anders Ericsson, it takes ten thousand hours to become an expert at something, whether that's math, or learning a new instrument, speaking another language … or bootstrapping. It's important to remember this as you take the first steps in your career. There's always a learning curve when you're looking for your first full-time job. You will often ask yourself if you're doing things right, if you're coming off as trying too hard, overselling yourself, or even underselling yourself. Hell, maybe you don't know where to start. What I want you to do when those feelings come up is flush them away. You wouldn't show up to your first piano lesson and beat yourself up for not being able to play a symphony, would you? Don't expect to be an expert hustler right from the jump. Things may not go your way right away, and that's fine.

The important thing to take away is that each interview, each rejection, each and every application is an opportunity to learn. Having the mindset of always learning is an essential component to bootstrapping. You can try different methods, test different styles, and generally treat each application as an experiment. Think of it like the scientist testing a thousand methods to find the one that is the cure. Or if you're more of a sports guy, consider it to be a bit like the game of baseball. Even the greats fail seven out of ten times at bat (or more!). So if you send out ten applications, you might get three phone interviews, and only one "home run"—the in-person (or Zoom) interview. It will take even more at bats to hit the grand slam, (the job)!

Bootstrapping, like everything in life, is a learned skill, which means it takes practice, and the best way to practice something is to build it into your daily routine. Don't think of it as a separate thing—something you can do once in a while and then be done with. That's a mistake, because the *best opportunities come when you're not actively looking for them.* In order to be prepared for these opportunities when they come, you need to prepare yourself by making some specific lifestyle choices. For example, you should cultivate an executive presence in all aspects for your daily life. We will talk more about this throughout the book, but for now, you should consider this to be a professional attitude and confidence, even when under pressure or when you are feeling the least confident. (If you want to learn a bit more about this in general terms now, I recommend checking out this article on BetterUp by Shonna Water—"Why You Need Executive Presence (And How To Get It).")[19] If you make bootstrapping a lifestyle, instead of a chore, you'll keep yourself open to opportunities that aren't as obvious.

What does this look like in practice?

- **Set aside some time every day for *hunting*.** I'm talking about *dedicated, distraction-free* time. Turn off your ringer, log out of your social media, and tell your roommates to shut up. It doesn't have to be for a long time. Even ten or fifteen minutes a day will add up. Whenever you find a lead, make a note of it.

- **Set aside some additional time every day for *applying*.**
  Make sure to do this separately from when you're searching
  for jobs. Maybe you search for ten minutes each evening,
  and then apply for ten minutes each morning for the
  jobs you found the previous night. It's important to keep
  these things separate, since they involve being in two
  different headspaces.
- **Stay consistent.** This is the big one. Figure out what you
  have the time and energy for and *keep doing it*. If you can,
  do it at the same time every day. Once you've decided how
  much time you have to dedicate, consider setting a timer.
  When it goes off, you're done. What you want to avoid is
  getting burnt out on the first mile of the marathon and
  running out of gas when you approach the finish line.
- **Discipline is the key.** Think of job-hunting like going to
  the gym. You don't get in shape from one session. Maybe
  at first you can only lift ten pounds. Then, as you make it a
  habit, you start to get stronger. Ten pounds becomes twenty,
  and then fifty. The longer you stick with it, the easier it gets.

FIGURE OUT WHAT MOTIVATES YOU

Inertia kills dreams. It's a fact. I'm as guilty of it as anyone.

Getting started is always the trickiest part of any big task, and
that goes beyond just looking for a job. You see something challenging, and you balk. It's a universal human trait. I like to think of it as
climbing a mountain: you stand at the trailhead at four o'clock in the
morning, looking up at the summit way off in the distance, and it's
easy to psych yourself out. "How the hell am I supposed to do this?
How is *anyone* supposed to do this?" It's tempting to go back to your
car, drive home, and crawl back into bed. You forget that climbing a

mountain is actually a pretty simple task in theory. All you have to do is put one foot in front of the other.

Getting a job is the same. How can you get motivated for something that isn't even guaranteed? You're staring at dozens of applications and just as many rejections—if they even bother to reject you and don't just ghost you completely. Why even bother at all, and even if you do, why put in effort?

It's a conundrum, and it's a bigger problem now than ever before. Study after study has shown that our attention spans have taken a nosedive in recent years due to the internet, social media, and need for instant gratification. This has caused problems for our motivation and ability to dig into involved tasks—especially tasks that don't have an immediate reward. If that doesn't describe job hunting, then I don't know what does.

So how do you get around this, especially when you're already swamped with school, a part-time job, an internship, and a social life? *You have to find your own motivation.* Start by thinking about what immediately inspires you. Some people start their day with a workout. Some people meditate. Others prefer to go for walks, take (short) naps, read an engaging book, or do something creative. Whatever it is, find a way to incorporate it into the bootstrapping process. If you need to reward yourself after an hour of sending out résumés, do it. If you have to go for a jog to clear your mind and reset your headspace before you sit down to apply, go for it. Figure out what works for you, and what will help you sustain your mission.

Now think about what motivates you *long-term*. What's your end goal? Think about launching your career as the first step toward that goal. If becoming the CEO of a company is the Super Bowl, then getting your first job is trying out for your college team. You won't find fame and glory right away, but you'll be one step closer to reaching the top. For the purposes of this book, we are going to focus on the next three, five, and ten years. However, if you feel inspired to think beyond that, absolutely do it. Having an end goal for thirty years from now will never hurt. Just keep in mind that this goal may change as you continue down your career path. Here are a couple ways to stoke your motivation.

- **Write down your career goals.** Think about the classic question, "Where do you see yourself in five years? Ten years?" You can make this as detailed as you want, as long as it gets you excited for the future. Draw pictures. Photoshop yourself onto the cover of *Forbes*. Whatever inspires you. Post these goals somewhere you can see them whenever you're sitting down to work.

- **Identify your career role models.** Who has your desired success story? This doesn't have to be some big-name billionaire; it could be your father, who worked his way to success from the ground up. It could be the person who owns the most successful small business in your hometown, or someone in your life who has turned their passions into a lasting career.

  Also think about successful people whose story started out the same way yours did. Who had to hustle to get where they are today? Who went to the same college as you did? Who was born in the same city? By finding people you can identify with who made it to where you want to be, the path to victory becomes a little less daunting.

- **Determine Your Career Dealbreakers.** In the new hybrid workplace, you will probably be allowed to work from home at least part time. Is that enough? Do you want to be fully remote? How important is having flexible hours? What kind of benefits package do you need? How far are you willing to commute? What aren't you willing to negotiate on? How will a hybrid workplace affect the jobs you are applying for and how will you handle that?

These are all questions you need to genuinely consider. They will help you as you determine which jobs you'd like to apply for, and, bonus, they may even pop up as interview questions!

THE OPPORTUNITY IN RISK

Another factor to consider in the planning stage is your willingness to take risks. Entering the workforce for the first time, or even re-entering it after time away, provides you with the opportunity to take bigger risks. Perhaps working for the big, stable company isn't the best option for you. Maybe working for the small startup that you're passionate about is the better choice.

Sure, you probably won't be paid as much. And the benefits may suck. But there could also be huge opportunities for growth, or stock options, or other benefits that just might be worth the risk—especially if it is a company in which you really believe. One year down the road, you could already be in a managerial role with full benefits and a big raise. On the flip side, the company could go bust and you end up with nothing but the experience. It's a risk. But that's what makes it exciting!

It's also an opportunity to find impact. What I mean by that is you could find a company that makes a difference. Something you're passionate about. It's all a compromise.

Let me give you an example. This is a story from my friend, Brad Johnson. He is the former Vice President of Wayfair and is now a professor at Babson College (my alma mater!). Brad had a student who was very into cars. Let's call him Henry. Henry just wanted to work in a car company. He applied to several programs at Ford and BMW and was very disappointed when he didn't get them. But Brad told him, "You don't want to work at those companies. Everything they do is very much already figured out. You'd probably do a good job and they'd be lucky to have you, but you won't make as much *impact*." Brad told him he should look into Tesla or Lucid Motors, or some new electric car company.

Henry followed Brad's advice and found a wonderful job at one of those (then) smaller companies that is doing cutting edge work. In just eighteen months, he's been promoted three times and is now their supply chain manager. As Brad says himself, if Henry had gone to Ford or one of the big companies, he would have been lost in the overall size, structure, process, and red tape. At big companies like that they have annual promotion processes and schedules and other things that would have kept Henry from being as engaged as he could be, and thus unable to make as much of an impact. He would never have risen so quickly in a traditional corporate structure. Working in a smaller company also gave Henry the opportunity to make some impactful decisions within his team that provided him immediate experiences that he would not have otherwise been given. Henry took a risk to have the impact he wanted in the industry he loved, and it paid off—big time!

I love stories like this. Most people do. We find them inspirational and aspirational. We all want to have a success story of our own, and the perfect time to take a risk like Henry's is when you are just getting out of college and have the ability to go with the early-stage and fast-growing companies. *But only if you're comfortable with the risks associated.* Just like entrepreneurship, this is something you need to carefully assess about yourself. It's not for everyone and many people are far more comfortable staying in the corporate structure and going for slow, steady, and safe growth. And that's a completely valid choice, too. Now is the time to prepare your own personal risk assessment.

#PACE PROCESS STEPS

- **Train your hustle muscle, and don't let it atrophy.** Build job-searching into your daily routine, for as much time as you can spare. Keep this time separate and consistent. Same goes for keeping a special time for applying.
- **Figure out what motivates you.** What drives you? What gets you going? Find a way to leverage it to inspire you. Remember, it's only by starting from where you are that you'll end up where you want to be.
- **Lean into the uncertainty.** The job search is intimidating, but don't shy away from it. Concentrate on what's in your control and look at every rejection as a step toward that golden opportunity.
- **Do a Risk-Level Analysis.** Determine what level of risk you're willing to entertain, what the tradeoffs are, and what you're passionate about. Consider if going for impact is important to you. If you have the option to do so, take the risk. It may just pay off big.

CHAPTER 3
LEVERAGING A NETWORK

YOU'VE NOW INCORPORATED THE RIGHT MINDSET and bootstrapping into your life. Great. But what are you looking for? I keep using this word, "opportunity." What *is* opportunity, and how the hell are you supposed to find it? Why is knowing where to look so important? Well, it isn't so much knowing where to look as it is being open to opportunities and accepting that the linear path may not be an option. Embrace out-of-the-box thinking.

Consider the following example: Andy, who is searching for a new job, finds an opening at a company where he's always wanted to work. The only catch is that the open position isn't what he's looking for. Maybe it's in a different department than the one where he wants to work, or it's a step down from his current role. Even though this is his dream company, it's not his dream job, so he passes on applying and turns to searching elsewhere without thinking about less-straightforward ways of getting what he wants.

Now consider Beth, who sees that opening and jumps on it. Sure, it isn't the role she originally wanted, but she also understands the opportunity of getting her foot in the door. She understands that once she's integrated into her dream company, there will be more connections and opportunities than she could possibly find from the outside. She decides to take the job, even though it's not her dream job, and once she's in, she works her way up to the role she really does want. Now she's working her dream job at her dream company, and it's all because she understood that opportunity doesn't always lie in the obvious places.

AREN'T JOB LISTINGS ENOUGH?

This is the obvious question, isn't it? It feels like a no-brainer. You open LinkedIn, Indeed, Monster, etc., type in the role you want, and skim the listings. Did you find exactly what you were looking for? Great! More power to you. I'm not trying to talk you out of traditional job hunting. In fact, it can be a great starting point… if you're qualified and motivated enough to get noticed. This is just another reason why being focused and consistent with your searches is extremely important: all you're doing by half-assing it is selling yourself short, especially when there's already so much competition.

All that said, I would be doing you a disservice to just give you advice for online job-hunting, especially when there are better methods out there. I want to help you score a touchdown, not a field goal.

Did you know that 80 percent of jobs aren't posted on job boards?[20] If the job market is an iceberg, then the bulk of its size is what's under the water. By sticking to the 20 percent that's above the surface, you're setting yourself up for fierce competition with everyone else who doesn't think to look beyond the obvious. You should also consider the fact that a large portion of the jobs that *do* get posted on job boards will still end up going to people who already work at the company via internal promotion. Wouldn't you rather have the job come to you, instead of the other way around? Wouldn't it be nice not to have to duke it out with everyone else on the internet?

If most jobs for hire aren't going to the people applying online, who are they going to? They're going to the people who network. You had to have known this was coming, right? Everyone talks about how important networking is because it's more effective and more productive than scouring the internet, and (this may surprise you) it's *easier.* Quality networking can mean the difference between spending three months searching on job boards and one month talking to the right people. For a generation that grew up with the internet, it's pretty easy to overlook this, but it can be your ticket in.

NETWORKING 101
WHAT IS A NETWORK?

It depends on who you ask. I like to define it as a community, whether virtual or in-person, of working professionals who share advice, leads, and resources with one another in a symbiotic relationship. Contrary to what some say, your network doesn't have to have a singular field or focus. In fact, I believe that the more diverse your network is, the more potential it holds to bring you—and others—tangible success.

WHAT YOUR NETWORK CAN DO FOR YOU.

Remember when I said opportunity isn't always obvious? This is what I was talking about. First of all, one of the key words is symbiotic. Your network is your opportunity to find people who can help you, but you should also be using it to help others when you can. You may not have much power to do this initially, but this goes back to mindset. If you go into networking with the mindset of helping others as much, or more, than they help you, your networking success will likely increase exponentially.

People in your network probably aren't going to call you out of the blue and offer you a job. That's why you need to keep your feelers out at all times and constantly seek to expand your network. Here are two examples of what I like to call "opportunities in disguise."

- **"A friend of a friend ..."** It's extremely important to touch base with your connections every once in a while. Often, even if they don't currently have anything for you at their own company, they'll know someone at a different company who does. And if you've maintained a strong professional relationship with them, they will likely be willing to pass your name along. By keeping your name and background fresh in your contacts' minds, you can gain access to any opportunities that crop up in *their* networks, as well as your own. Every connection you maintain can lead to exponentially more connections, creating a spiderweb of possibilities.

- **"Do you know anyone who ...?"** The more useful you are to your network, the more useful your network will be to you. Perhaps someone you know is looking to fill a position you're not qualified for. Sure, you could ignore it, but the smarter path is to give them any recommendations you may have. Offer to put them in touch with anyone you know who you honestly believe would be suitable for the job. Even if nothing comes of it, when you go above and beyond for the people in your circle, they're more likely to reciprocate. Symbiosis, remember? This could mean notifying you of an open position, putting you in touch with other influential people, or vouching for you when the time comes.

WHO SHOULD BE IN YOUR NETWORK?

For starters, I don't believe in filtering your network. If you want to be a journalist, and you have connections in medicine, your first instinct might be not to bother maintaining a relationship with them. I think this is a mistake. Never turn down the opportunity to add someone to your network, even if they aren't involved in your field. You never know when a dietician is going to need a freelance writer, or when a counselor is going to need a web designer. Or when you will be writing an article on either subject and need an expert to interview.

That said, prioritizing your network connections is important, especially when you're just starting out:

There are three types of connections to consider when you build your network.

- **Immediate connections:** These are people you've met and associated with previously. Professors, former managers, colleagues, collaborators, friends, and family. They will form the basis of your network.
- **One step removed:** These are connections you make through other people or circumstances. Maybe they're people whom you've never met, but who worked at the same company as you. Maybe they're friends-of-friends, distant relatives, or workers in your same niche. In general, you'll probably be communicating with these connections less frequently.
- **Remote connections:** These are people to whom you have no prior connection—think of people you meet at conferences, workshops, classes, events, or by random chance.

If you think about your professional network like social media, then you'll likely be interacting with and paying most attention to your immediate connections. These are the connections you want to dedicate the most time to nurturing and cultivating, but that doesn't mean you should ignore those other ones. You have to be decisive about where you put your energy as you network.

This is where LinkedIn can come into play more than any other network. This is your professional social media profile, and you should keep it purely professional. This is the profile you should keep public, be very judicious about what you post on it, and make sure to *make all other social media profiles private.* The first thing your network and, indeed, hiring managers will do is check out your social media profile. And while I'm sure that frat party beer pong tournament was a lot of fun, it is not the first thing you want potential network connections or hiring managers to see.

This is also especially important as we move into the hybrid workplace. Virtual networking is becoming more and more standard. There are all kinds of connections we make virtually and those connections can lead to jobs. I know several people who connected to others in their industry solely by LinkedIn and email communication, and when they were looking for a specific job, their connection just happened to know the perfect position. It happens! All because of LinkedIn and email.

STRATEGIES FOR BUILDING YOUR NETWORK

- **Look for chances to meet other professionals.** Job conferences and retreats, job fairs, and professional meetups are a great place to start. Also consider school events, volunteering opportunities, hobby groups, religious or cultural groups and events, online forums, alumni meetups, and so on. If you'll run into other working people there, odds are it's a good place to network.

- **Make yourself easy to remember.** Introducing yourself is great, but when the person you're talking to has already met a dozen other people in the last hour, you'll want to do something to keep yourself fresh in their mind. Consider making up some business cards describing who you are, what you do, and how to best contact you.

- **Practice your "elevator pitch."** Pretend you only have thirty seconds to concisely explain yourself to a prospective connection. Who are you? What's your background? What are you looking for, but more importantly, *what do you have to offer other people?* Speak in broad, easy-to-understand terms, and remember to #Pace yourself. Talk slowly and clearly—this isn't about getting your whole life story out in less than a minute. It's about emphasizing the most interesting and relevant parts of your background. The trick here is to sell yourself without "selling yourself." If you were the person listening, what would be the most important takeaways?

Here's an example elevator pitch: "I'm a digital content writer, focused on the health and wellness industry. Being a fitness enthusiast, I am passionate about working with companies that genuinely want to help their customers, and I strive to promote company brands in a way that feels fun and authentic. I believe this is an important element in forming a relationship with an audience that will keep them engaged long-term."

You'll notice this pitch is short, sweet, and to the point, describing what this person does, what they specialize in, and how they use their understanding of the industry to benefit their employers. They also manage to work in a couple of their interests (health and wellness) in the context of why they're a unique fit for the work they do. This helps them stand out while keeping the "fun facts" relevant to their professional background.

- **Start with what you can do for others, not what they can do for you.** It's easy to jump right in with, "I need a job," or "I'm looking for a role that has X, Y, and Z." Don't. Neediness is a turn-off. Instead, approach the situation from a point of view of "what does this other person need? What are they looking for?" If you can't fill that void right now, try to put them in touch with someone who can. Odds are, they'll remember you better when something *does* eventually come up that they could offer you.

  It doesn't even have to be work-related. If someone mentions looking for a new hairdresser or dentist, feel free to give them a recommendation. Take any chance you have to be open and generous, and at the end of the conversation, make sure to reiterate that you're at their disposal. It doesn't have to sound kiss-assy. All you have to do is finish up with, "Feel free to reach out if there's anything you need," and make sure you have those business cards handy. Always view communication as a two-way street; if you can offer value to the other person, through your actions or your words, then you should. It could be anything from a business connection to a restaurant recommendation, as long as you offer it in good faith. Sincerity is the key to game.

- **Listen and ask questions.** No one likes listening to someone who rambles on about themselves. A conversation is a two-way-street, which means you'll need to give as much as you take. Focus first and foremost on forging a genuine human connection. Engage with what the other person is saying, and don't always try to redirect the conversation back to yourself. Ask questions and make sure the person who you're communicating with feels heard.

The more dynamic you can make the exchange, the more possibilities that can turn into opportunities. You may even end up on an issue that is relevant to you and your skillset.

- **Follow up.** Touching base after you first meet someone is a great way to make sure you develop a relationship. Take some time later that day to shoot them an email thanking them for their time, reiterating that it was a pleasure to meet them, and reminding them to reach out if there's anything you can do for them. If you offer to do anything for anyone, whether it's connecting them with someone else or proofreading a cover letter, do it, and do it in a timely manner. Assuming it's appropriate, follow-up with them a few days later to check in and see how they're doing. Make sure they know that you valued their time and the opportunity to get to know them.

- **Never burn bridges.** Your former bosses and ex-coworkers are often some of the most important people you can leverage in your network. This might sound counterintuitive, especially when it comes to former employers. After all, if you left a job, why bother staying in touch with the people from your old company? But think about it: Who understands your skills, strengths, goals, and accomplishments better than those who have seen them firsthand? They could be references for future job applications or potential collaborators on future projects, and they may even be your ticket to a better role at your old company.

After you build your network, make sure to reach out to your connections every once in a while to ask them how they're doing, get a sense of their current needs, and keep yourself fresh in their memory. If they post content on LinkedIn, engage with it; take the time to comment or like their post to keep your name in their notification list and on their mind. Remember, this is about what *you* can do for *them*, not the other way around.

The most obvious benefits of networking are the job opportunities, but they don't stop there. By building a presence and positive reputation within your network, you're opening up doors that would otherwise be closed. Maybe someone will write you a wonderful reference or maybe they're starting their own company and want you on board. Maybe they will want to interview you, bring you on as a consultant, mentor you, sponsor you, invest in your growth… the possibilities are endless and go miles beyond what a simple job posting can do for you.

FOR THOSE WITH SOCIAL ANXIETY

I know all this can seem intimidating. Especially if you're an introvert. This can be a tricky thing, and as an extrovert myself, I may not necessarily have personal experience. However, I have a deep respect for the unique talents of introverts. Research shows that introverts are extremely valuable to the workplace. But getting the job can be more difficult for them, especially in this networking stage. As you read the previous sections in this chapter, I bet there are more than a few of you who said to yourself, "Oh, no. I could never do that. I'd be too shy/nervous/scared/whatever." But you have to push through that feeling. Just consider this an opportunity to grow.

Here's the thing. You can't skimp on this networking step. Not if you are really committed to finding success and your dream job. I understand that it is uncomfortable, so start with the steps that are easier for you and work up from there. In the spirit of that, here are a few tips to help you learn to overcome these fears.

- **Prepare talking points.** Being prepared can help ease anxiety.[21] We talked about an elevator pitch earlier, but you can prepare other talking points, too. How are you going to introduce yourself? What are some "small talk" openers?
- **Practice a script.** Enlist your friends and family to help you practice. Prepare a little script. Be prepared to deviate from this script but having it as a starting point will help. This might look something like:
  - Introduction: Say "Hello. My name is John Doe. [They respond.] It's nice to meet you."
  - Opener: Ask a question. "What brings you to this networking event tonight?" [They just moved to the area.]
  - Follow up: "Welcome to Boston! What brought you out here?" [A job at Company XYZ.]
  - Response: "That's great! It's a wonderful company. How do you like it so far? I've been looking at applying there myself."
  - Continue conversation.
  - Goodbye: Say "It was great meeting you. I hope we can stay in touch on LinkedIn. I'll send an invite."
- **Remember Your Body Language.** It really is true that faking confidence can increase your confidence.[22] Prepping the right outfit that makes you feel your most attractive and confident is one step in the right direction. Going in with

the right mindset helps even more. Even if you feel like an imposter, faking confidence will appear genuine to others. Fake it 'til you make it.

These tips aren't new or novel, but they are a few of the most effective ones that seem to work for introverts I know. You may have to find your own methods that work for *you*. But the key isn't what or how you do it. It's that you get started on the process of networking. Do the work to create the network and maintain it as a lifestyle and mindset, even when it's hard. Practice these tips every day, and even if you are not an extrovert, they will start to feel more natural. Start with one step each day and add from there. By the end, you will be a networking pro and this be will an easy task for the rest of your career!

#PACE PROCESS STEPS

- **Prep your social media now.** Turn all your social media profiles to PRIVATE except LinkedIn. Be careful in what you post on all social media, but especially LinkedIn. Keep LinkedIn professional and use it as a platform to start networking virtually.
- **Network, network, network.** Always have your eyes peeled for chances to meet other working people. Keep your networking hat on no matter where you are. If someone needs something, try to be the one to provide it to them. Keep track of your connections and get in touch with them periodically.
- **Be genuine.** Sincerity is essential. Be genuine in your desire to help others as much as they help you. Pay it forward. Reciprocity is the name of the game.

- **Practice your talking points.** Practice makes perfect. Whether you suffer from social anxiety or are uber-confident, practice will help everyone. Practice your elevator pitch, practice your small talk, and practice confidence. It will go a long way, I promise.

APPLY

#PACE: PREPARE + **APPLY** + COMMIT + EXPLORE

NOW THAT YOU'VE DEVELOPED THE RIGHT MINDSET, set up a schedule for yourself, scrubbed your online presence, and started networking, you need to develop the tools to start applying. Just like networking, this step can't be skipped. It all feeds into who you are as a person and as a professional—your brand. You are building your executive presence, and for that you need a top-notch résumé, cover letter, and interview skills. Getting the job you want is one of the more challenging things you will do in life, and it all starts with putting together an attractive package for your potential employer. With the new realities of applicant tracking systems (ATS) and the expectations of hybrid workspaces, the traditional application process has changed a bit in the last year, but certain aspects still hold true.

I've always believed that the power of networking is greater than that of a mass-mailing résumés. I stand by this assertion, but I also acknowledge that résumés and cover letters play an important role. You really can't have one without the other. They all speak to your brand. The Brand of You. It's time you really sit down and think what that will be. You don't need all the answers. You don't need the perfect job. You don't need to know the meaning of life, either. But you do need to start crafting your brand and how it will help you achieve your goals. This will change over the years, and that's the way it's supposed to be.

The big thing I want to emphasize here is to apply: Apply to jobs, sure, but most importantly apply yourself. Apply yourself to your job, to this process, to building your brand as an employee, and to doing things the right way. Apply yourself with the same focus as you would any social media picture, post, or story.

CHAPTER 4

PERSONAL BRAND, RÉSUMÉS, & COVER LETTERS

THE HYBRID MODEL

Let's revisit this idea of the "Hybrid Model." What does this mean for the workforce? We will talk a bit more about working in a hybrid office, but there are also considerations for applying to a company you know is utilizing a hybrid workspace or even a fully remote one.

COVID-19 has accelerated the change of the workplace forever. Companies had to scramble to adjust their offices and how they conduct business throughout the shutdown. This meant a lot of things were done arbitrarily. Quick and ugly, they were a Band-aid on the problem. But that is changing. Companies have now had a year to assess and research the issue. Many are choosing to stay remote, or to offer various remote options for their employees. This absolutely affects their hiring practices, and that's important for you to know.

Let's discuss this a bit further. Say you're a hiring manager looking to fill a position that was previously in the office, but now is at least partially done remotely. What do you think the hiring manager will be looking for in an applicant? It's not just about having the skills of the job anymore. There will not be a supervisor looking over your shoulder making sure you do your work. They need to know that you get your work done on your own. That you have good time-management skills. Maybe that you are efficient at typing and other computer skills. They may also be looking for strong communication skills—do you write in a professional tone and manner. Do you communicate well with both clients and colleagues? Are you skilled at communicating by phone and on virtual meetings (Zoom, Webex, and so on). This is a skill that need to be showcased in a résumé. Do your research. Learn about the company, their needs, and try to anticipate the questions they might ask about working in a hybrid or remote environment.

RÉSUMÉS

We've finally made it to the big one—résumés, known as a curriculum vitae (CV) when the emphasis is on academic credentials. This is the first big piece to your executive presence, to your brand. There is a lot of advice out there about résumés and there are a lot of résumé writing services. I'm not going to go into that level of detail here because they can offer more detailed advice specific to your industry and/or career stage. Instead, we are going to look at some examples, discuss a few things to keep in mind about your approach, but most of all, we will discuss how this will build into your personal brand.

Let's look at an example to get started. First, let's start with the job posting. Our imaginary example is for a Project Management Assistant.

You'll notice that these are not short posts anymore; companies, more often than not, add in quite a bit of detail.

JOB DESCRIPTION

Do you love to organize complicated projects and manage busy schedules? Are you passionate about helping people find their way in a new company? Do you love to impact how people experience their company culture? As the Project Management Assistant at Company XYZ, you'll be a key member within our Human Resources team! This team is dedicated to developing and maintaining programming that improves our employees' work experience. The HR team seeks an assistant adept at organizational and administrative support to help manage these employee programs

KEY RESPONSIBILITIES

- *Support department managers with the organization and execution of content for each of the company's resource groups.*
- *Help manage the budget allocation and account management of an employee recognition program.*
- *Oversee the quality assurance and execution of a peer-to-peer public recognition program.*
- *Recruit team members to participate in and administer a program to support new hires joining the company.*
- *Facilitate new-hire resource kit ordering and delivery.*
- *Communicate with new hires about onboarding and manage their schedules.*
- *Provide scheduling support for special programming.*

REQUIRED QUALIFICATIONS

- *Degree in human resources management, business analytics, statistics, or other related experience.*

PREFERRED QUALIFICATIONS

- *History of exhibiting attention to the little things and relaying detailed information to various audiences.*
- *Excellent at communication and presentation skills (verbal and written).*
- *Able to multitask and work in a fast-paced, collaborative team environment.*
- *Experienced in organizing complicated projects with multiple moving parts and targets.*
- *Familiar with survey, database, and calendar tools.*
- *Creative with a point of view, but always open to new ideas and collaborating closely with a cross-functional team.*
- *Excited to solve unique and challenging problems.*
  Company XYZ is an equal employment opportunity employer, committed to an inclusive workplace. We do not discriminate on the basis of race, sex, gender, national origin, religion, sexual orientation, gender identity, marital or familial status, age, ancestry, disability, genetic information, or any other characteristic protected by applicable laws. We believe in diversity and encourage all qualified individuals to apply.

Next, let's look at a sample résumé. This is a real résumé from a real student who volunteered to be a part of this book. She provided her résumé for a before and after assessment which we shared with her for future personal use as well.

A N
student@school.edu   (123) 456-7890

Babson College, School of Business   Wellesley, MA
Bachelor of Science in Business Administration May 2023
Concentrations in Strategic Management and Operations Management
Relevant Coursework Foundations of Management and Entrepreneurship, Microeconomics, Macroeconomics, Business Analytics, Financial Accounting, Managerial Accounting, Operations Management, Business Law, Project Management, Principles of Marketing, IT, Principles of Finance, Retailing Management, Supply Chain Management, Sustainable Operations, Strategic Problem Solving

Experience
Business Administration & Operations Intern Capital Cartridge   June - August 2021
Conducted cost analysis and market research to reduce company spending on office and warehouse services, saving over $3,000 in monthly services such as janitorial, waste removal, uniform rental, and drinking water. Researched product price comparisons with competitors and worked to update and redesign the brand's B2C retail site. Implemented office floor plan rearrangement, accommodating collaborative work efforts between employees.

Peer Mentor Babson College   July 2020 - Present
Supporting Babson College in achieving the goals of transition and retention for new students through Undergraduate Orientation and the First-Year Seminar program. Facilitating discussions and educational content, and providing one-on-one support and mentorship to cohort members.

FME Mentor/Teaching Assistant Babson College   August 2020 - Present
Collaborating with two professors, facilitating and mentoring students through Babson College's flagship course, Foundations of Management and Entrepreneurship, covering entrepreneurship, marketing, accounting, organizational behavior, information systems, and operations over the course of a year.

VP of Membership Sigma Kappa Zeta Zeta, Babson College   November 2020 - January 2022
Overseeing Sigma Kappa's recruitment planning and logistics implementation processes, engaging with 80+ chapter members to teach recruiting techniques, leading and delegating a committee of chapter members, and planning and managing over twenty chapter membership and recruiting events.

Chief Operating Officer ContraBands Co., Babson College   November 2019 - April 2020
As part of a twelve member team within a school-funded program, purchased and oversaw the selling of product and inventory (customized woven bracelets), ran meetings, presented weekly updates, and assisted in finances and marketing of the venture. Revenue of over $1,070 in the first month, profits donated to Hope and Comfort, Boston based charitable organization.

Intern WatchHerWork, Houston, TX   April 2018 - August 2019
Worked alongside WatchHerWork Founder and CEO, Denise Hamilton, learning about entrepreneurship, managing social media, coordinating events, and designing slide decks.

Campus Engagement
Sigma Kappa Zeta Zeta, Babson College
Social sorority dedicated to philanthropy, and social and intellectual development
Housing Manager May 2020-Present
Babson Hillel Foundation for Jewish Campus Life and Cultural Engagement
President August 2020-January 2021
Community Service Over 900 hours in Food Banks, Blood Drives, and other organizations

Skills
- Proficient in Microsoft Office, Microsoft Project, QuickBooks and Tableau
- Leadership, Team Work, Problem Solving, Public Speaking, and Conflict Resolution
- Fluent Hebrew, Intermediate Spanish

A***** N*****
STUDENT@SCHOOL.EDU (123) 456-7890

BABSON COLLEGE, SCHOOL OF BUSINESS   Wellesley, MA

Bachelor of Science in Business Administration May 2023

Concentrations in Strategic Management and Operations Management

RELEVANT COURSEWORK Foundations of Management and Entrepreneurship, Microeconomics, Macroeconomics, Business Analytics, Financial Accounting, Managerial Accounting, Operations Management, Business Law, Project Management, Principles of Marketing, IT, Principles of Finance, Retailing Management, Supply Chain Management, Sustainable Operations, Strategic Problem Solving

EXPERIENCE

Business Administration & Operations Intern

Capital Cartridge   June - August 2021

Conducted cost analysis and market research to reduce company spending on office and warehouse services, saving over $3,000 in monthly services such as janitorial, waste removal, uniform rental, and drinking water. Researched product price comparisons with competitors and worked to update and redesign the brand's B2C retail site. Implemented office floor plan rearrangement, accommodating collaborative work efforts between employees.

PEER MENTOR BABSON COLLEGE   July 2020 - Present

Supporting Babson College in achieving the goals of transition and retention for new students through Undergraduate Orientation and the First-Year Seminar program. Facilitating discussions and educational content, and providing one-on-one support and mentorship to cohort members.

FME MENTOR/TEACHING ASSISTANT

Babson College   August 2020 - Present

Collaborating with two professors, facilitating and mentoring students through Babson College's flagship course, Foundations of Management and Entrepreneurship, covering entrepreneurship, marketing, accounting, organizational behavior, information systems, and operations over the course of a year.

VP OF MEMBERSHIP
Sigma Kappa Zeta Zeta, Babson College November 2020 - January 2022
Overseeing Sigma Kappa's recruitment planning and logistics implementation processes, engaging with 80+ chapter members to teach recruiting techniques, leading and delegating a committee of chapter members, and planning and managing over twenty chapter membership and recruiting events.

CHIEF OPERATING OFFICER Contra Bands Co., Babson College
November 2019 - April 2020
As part of a twelve member team within a school-funded program, purchased and oversaw the selling of product and inventory (customized woven bracelets), ran meetings, presented weekly updates, and assisted in finances and marketing of the venture. Revenue of over $1,070 in the first month, profits donated to Hope and Comfort, Boston based charitable organization.

INTERN WatchHerWork, Houston, TX   April 2018 - August 2019
Worked alongside WatchHerWork Founder and CEO, Denise Hamilton, learning about entrepreneurship, managing social media, coordinating events, and designing slide decks.

CAMPUS ENGAGEMENT
SIGMA KAPPA ZETA ZETA, Babson College
Social sorority dedicated to philanthropy, and social and intellectual development
Housing Manager May 2020-Present

Babson Hillel Foundation for Jewish Campus Life and
Cultural Engagement
President August 2020-January 2021
Community Service Over 900 hours in Food Banks, Blood Drives, and
other organizations

Skills

- Proficient in Microsoft Office, Microsoft Project, QuickBooks
and Tableau
- Leadership, Team Work, Problem Solving, Public Speaking, and
Conflict Resolution
- Fluent Hebrew, Intermediate Spanish

What do you notice about it? Visually plain? Maybe a little hard to read or too compressed in spacing? How about the fact that it doesn't showcase clear achievements or skills that are easily identifiable? On an even more micro level, ATS systems likely wouldn't pick up the right keywords because it's not focused to the specific job posting. This résumé could easily get lost in the sea of applicants. It lacks the detail necessary to fully explain her role in various positions and the value she contributed.

Let's look at a few aspects you need to be aware of as you write your résumé. These are just brief reviews. When in doubt, do a little extra research into each before finalizing your own résumé.

APPLICANT TRACKING SYSTEMS (ATS)

ATS software allows companies to quickly filter through résumés. They are useful for a company but can make things more difficult for all applicants, regardless of your qualifications. If you don't present your employment information in a way that the program's algorithm can recognize, you will get passed over before a human ever looks at your résumé. There has been a lot of discussion and controversy surrounding these systems in recent years, but they should not be as feared as they seem to be. According to Scott Johnson, a People Operations Manager, while there are companies out there that use sophisticated ATS programs that employ machine learning, most companies can't afford it.[23] Instead, according to several experts, most use simpler programs that employ screening questions and keyword searches to sort applicants.[24] In fact, the Harvard Business School issued a report that found "ATS platforms are utilized by 99 percent of Fortune 500 companies, and 75 percent of the 760 US employers Harvard surveyed."[25] So assume every time you apply, your résumé is going to encounter an ATS. This is now the rule, not the exception. That being said, Alan Walker, a Talent Acquisition specialist, still maintains that most companies use the ATS initially, but still put eyes on the majority of résumés submitted.[26]

To outsmart the ATS program, you will need to do your research. I know, I know. I've said that a dozen times already. But research is so important. It goes back to that bootstrapping mindset. So let's look again at that job description. What keywords do you see? Don't look at just the skills section. Look at the whole of the post, and you might check out the company's website to find further keywords related to their culture or other values.

Here's what I've pulled out of that description in the order I found them. (You're on your own for researching the company's website, but you got it!)

- Organize
- Complicated projects
- Challenging problems
- Schedules/scheduling
- Management
- Developing and maintaining programming
- Organizational and administrative support
- Organization and execution

- Budget allocation
- Account management
- Quality assurance
- Recruit
- Administer
- Facilitate ordering and delivery
- Communicate/ communication
- Business analytics
- Statistics
- Attention to the little things/Details
- Presentation
- Fast-paced
- Multi-task
- Collaborative team
- Collaboration
- Survey, database, and calendar tools
- New Ideas
- Creative

Wow, that's a lot. You may not be able to fit all of those on your résumé, but you should certainly try to get as many of them as you can. According to Scott Johnson, you should try to "mirror the types of language, the processes, and the information that's in the job application itself. The language that's used in the job description is likely the language used by the organization internally, and likely the language which is used to filter for keywords (if that's the way that they do it.)"[27] Humans are creatures of habit. We tend to word things the same way over and over. You should also keep in mind that other words may be entered into the system as well—words that cover the values of the company or other goals they may have (like those regarding diversity, equity, and inclusion.) It can be overwhelming but take the time to put some thought into this. One trait Scott suggests incorporating is resiliency.[28] Even if your résumé does make it through to a real person, it will only be in front of them for fifteen to twenty seconds as they scan your résumé to make sure it has the skills they're looking for—the ATS helps them highlight those skills faster for easy review.[29]

One other point of note on "beating the ATS." There is a lot of advice out there on this, and some of it is *not good*. For example, I've heard it be recommended that you add an entire page filled with any and every keyword you could possibly think of and then change the text color to white. The ATS will supposedly then catch all those keywords and flag your résumé for human review. When a human looks at it or prints it out, it will just appear as a blank page. I'll admit this sounds like a clever idea. But it isn't. For one thing, hiring managers are on to tricks like this. But far more importantly, is this really the image you want to project to a company? That you're gaming the system? What if you're not qualified for the job? They're going to figure it out and it's not a professional look, nor is it entirely ethical. It does not contribute to *your* executive presence. Furthermore, as Alan Walker pointed out, "All of that could be recorded. It might be on your file within that company's ATS, which can act as a candidate management program as well. First thing a company will do with an applicant is see if you already have a file." Having a note for unprofessionalism is not going to help you. So dress for the job you want, but don't steal the suit to do it. People tend to remember things like that.

UPDATED RÉSUMÉ/CV

Let's look at an updated résumé now.

A* * * * *
N* * * * *

STUDENT@SCHOOL.EDU
(123) 456-7890
ANYTOWN, MA
LINKEDIN [LINK]

PROFILE

Business Administration undergraduate student focused on operational organization and strategic management with a passion for macro-level business analysis and troubleshooting underperforming teams.

SKILLS

- *Software:* Microsoft Office, Microsoft Project, QuickBooks, Tableau, & Calendar Management
- *Leadership:* Teamwork, Creativity, Communication, Collaboration, Problem Solving, Multi-tasking, & Conflict Resolution
- *Language Skills:* Fluent Hebrew & Intermediate Spanish.

WORK EXPERIENCE

Business Administration & Operations Intern, *Capital Cartridge*   Jun. – Aug. 2021
Conducted cost analysis and market research to reduce company spending on office and warehouse services. Supported team in updating and redesigning the brand's B2C retail site. Implemented office floor plan rearrangement to accommodate collaborative teamwork and increase employee engagement.
- *Key Accomplishment: Saved company an estimated $3,000 per month in operational costs.*

Intern, *WatchHerWork*   Apr. 2018 – Aug. 2019
Worked alongside WatchHerWork Founder and CEO, Denise Hamilton. Managed social media, scheduled and executed workplace events, and designed slide decks.

COLLEGIATE EXPERIENCE

VP of Membership, *Sigma Kappa Zeta Zeta, Babson College*   Nov. 2020 – Present
Oversaw Sigma Kappa's recruitment planning and logistics implementation processes. Engaged with 80+ chapter members to teach recruiting techniques. Led a committee of chapter members to plan and manage over twenty membership and recruiting events.
- *Key Accomplishments: Systemized the management of a membership calendar and budget. Personally recruited double the average number of new members.*

FME Mentor & Teaching Assistant, *Babson College*   Aug. 2020 – Present
Collaborated with two professors to facilitate and mentor students through Babson College's flagship course, Foundations of Management and Entrepreneurship (FME).
- *Key Accomplishment: 1 of only 10 selected as mentors out of 90 applicants for FME program. Selected as key student speaker at student recruitment event.*

Chief Operations Officer, *ContraBands Co., Babson College*   Nov. 2019 – April 2020
Member of a twelve-member team within a school-funded program. Facilitated ordering and deliver of inventory (customized woven bracelets), lead meetings, presented weekly updates, and assisted in finance management and marketing initiatives. 100% of proceeds benefitted Hope and Comfort, a Boston-based charitable organization.
- *Key Accomplishment: Consistently exceeded weekly sales goals, broke even by Week 3, and achieved profits of over $1,000 in just the first month.*

EDUCATION

Bachelor of Science, Business Administration, *Babson College, School of Business*   2023
Concentrations in Strategic Management and Operations Management

VOLUNTEER & COMMUNITY ENGAGEMENT

Peer Mentor, *Babson College*   Jul. 2020 – Present

Babson Hillel Foundation for Jewish Campus Life and Cultural Engagement, *President*   Aug. 2020 – Jan. 2021

Community Service, *900+ hours at food banks, blood drives, and other charitable organizations*   Sept. 2019 – Present

---

	student@school.edu
A*****	(123) 456-7890
	Anytown, MA
N*****	LinkedIn [Link]

PROFILE

Business Administration undergraduate student focused on operational organization and strategic management with a passion for macro-level business analysis and troubleshooting underperforming teams.

SKILLS

- Software: Microsoft Office, Microsoft Project, QuickBooks, Tableau, & Calendar Management
- Leadership: Teamwork, Creativity, Communication, Collaboration, Problem Solving, Multi-tasking, & Conflict Resolution
- Language Skills: Fluent Hebrew & Intermediate Spanish.

WORK EXPERIENCE

BUSINESS OPERATIONS INTERN, *CAPITAL CARTRIDGE*   JUN. – AUG. 2021

Conducted cost analysis and market research to reduce company spending on office and warehouse services. Supported team in updating and redesigning the brand's B2C retail site. Implemented office floor plan rearrangement to accommodate collaborative teamwork and increase employee engagement.

- ***Key Accomplishment:*** *Saved company an estimated $3,000 per month in operational costs.*

INTERN, *WATCHHERWORK*   APR. 2018 – AUG. 2019

Worked alongside WatchHerWork Founder and CEO, Denise Hamilton. Managed social media, scheduled and executed workplace events, and designed slide decks.

COLLEGIATE EXPERIENCE

VP OF MEMBERSHIP, *SIGMA KAPPA ZETA ZETA, BABSON COLLEGE*   NOV. 2020 – PRESENT

Oversaw Sigma Kappa's recruitment planning and logistics implementation processes. Engaged with 80+ chapter members to teach recruiting techniques. Led a committee of chapter members to plan and manage over twenty membership and recruiting events.

- *Key Accomplishments: Systemized the management of a membership calendar and budget. Personally recruited double the average number of new members.*

FME MENTOR & TEACHING ASSISTANT, *BABSON COLLEGE* AUG. 2020 – PRESENT

Collaborated with two professors to facilitate and mentor students through Babson College's flagship course, Foundations of Management and Entrepreneurship (FME).

- *Key Accomplishment: 1 of only 10 selected as mentors out of 90 applicants for FME program. Selected as key student speaker at student recruitment event.*

CHIEF OPERATIONS OFFICER, *CONTRABANDS CO., BABSON COLLEGE* NOV. 2019 – APRIL 2020

Member of a twelve-member team within a school-funded program. Facilitated ordering and deliver of inventory (customized woven bracelets), lead meetings, presented weekly updates, and assisted in finance management and marketing initiatives. 100% of proceeds benefitted Hope and Comfort, a Boston-based charitable organization.

- *Key Accomplishment:* Consistently exceeded weekly sales goals, broke even by Week 3, and achieved profits of over $1,000 in just the first month.

EDUCATION

BACHELOR OF SCIENCE, BUSINESS ADMINISTRATION,
BABSON COLLEGE, SCHOOL OF BUSINESS   2023
Concentrations in Strategic Management and Operations Management

VOLUNTEER & COMMUNITY ENGAGEMENT

PEER MENTOR, *BABSON COLLEGE*   JUL. 2020 – PRESENT
BABSON HILLEL FOUNDATION FOR JEWISH CAMPUS LIFE
AND CULTURAL ENGAGEMENT, *PRESIDENT*   AUG. 2020 – JAN. 2021
  COMMUNITY SERVICE, 900+ HOURS AT FOOD BANKS, BLOOD DRIVES, AND OTHER
CHARITABLE ORGANIZATIONS   SEPT. 2019 – PRESENT

As you can see in this example, active verbs are used and key achievements are highlighted. Her résumé has been rephrased to use the keywords found in the job post in an engaging way. You'll note that her current job is in present tense, while past jobs are in past tense, (which is a debatable technique, but seems like it is commonly accepted now.) Her education experience was lowered as it is less relevant than her work experience, and the relevant coursework section was removed entirely. Honestly, unless you graduate Summa Cum Laude, Magna Cum Laude, or Cum Laude, you don't need to mention your GPA or most other academic achievements (certain exclusions: prestigious awards, or honors that are related to your chosen industry). Once you hit the workforce, those just don't matter as much anymore. It's your work experience and the impact you have made in those roles that matter. Hiring managers want to know you can do the job you are hired to do and provide value to the company, not how good a test-taker you are.

Some other points to note are how this new version reframes A.N.'s experience to showcase other skills that *are* applicable to the job posting. This is especially important for those of you who have unusual skills. Perhaps you are returning to civilian work from the military. Or you're returning to work after a few years as a stay-at-home parent. Or perhaps you have experience in the volunteer world or in other applicable areas like diversity, equity, and inclusion. These skills are very useful to companies, but only if you know how to frame them in a way that they will understand and extrapolate how that could be useful to their company. For A.N., her experience in recruitment for her sorority has suddenly become valuable on her résumé. Just because a job or volunteer experience doesn't seem relevant at first glance, that doesn't mean it's not. Really think about what you accomplished at each role.

The key here is to be completely honest. If you don't have exact numbers for results, estimate them—but make it clear it is an estimate. Don't exaggerate, and definitely don't lie, just reframe this information in a different way so that the hiring manager can clearly see why it is relevant experience.

Let's look at a real-life example. This comes to us from a colleague of mine who has requested to stay anonymous. She has made many connections over the years at several companies. She once knew a young man who had been enlisted in the Army. For years, the man had been in charge of moving trucks. But he didn't think that made him qualified for much of anything. Except maybe with a trucking company. But he didn't want to return to that line of work.

With some investigation, when this Army veteran actually sat down and thought about what his job entailed, he was able to frame that information in a way Corporate America could understand. He described his job as "Planning and executing a transportation strategy in high-risk circumstances. Led team to implement emergency protocols to divert routes for safety and efficiency." What company wouldn't want someone who can plan strategies, make changes on the fly, and in a high-stress environment?

Now it's your turn. Do some thinking and figure out the best way to present your skills.

LINKEDIN AND SOCIAL MEDIA

We talked some about social media back in Section 1. You should have already set your profiles to private and scrubbed anything you don't want visible from public profiles. You can learn about a company you are applying to on social media, but they can learn about you, too. If you haven't done this step, STOP HERE AND DO IT NOW. Hopefully you have also started networking to a certain extent on LinkedIn.

Now that you have completed your résumé, you should also apply this same data to your LinkedIn profile. You may also need to add a few things that your résumé does not include. The first (and easiest) step to take is to make sure you have a complete profile. That means including a professional photo, headline, and description, as well as including all your job experience from your résumé.

When it comes to your profile description, consider how you can highlight what makes you unique, and how you can use your skills to benefit potential employers. Just saying, "I'm an experienced content writer working at ABC Company" doesn't pack nearly the same punch as saying, "I write strategic content to help companies build their image, expand their online presence, and drive consumer engagement. With over three years of experience in marketing in the XYZ industry, I use my intuition and unique voice to bring brands to the next level."

This is also a good opportunity to expand on your networking. Remember, networking is not a one-and-done process. You should continue to develop this skill throughout your entire career. To that end, ask previous employers or supervisors to add a review to your LinkedIn profile. Have them endorse your skills there, too. Make a point to engage with other people's posts. React to them, comment on them, and share relevant opinions. LinkedIn rewards users who make an effort to explore the site, so don't be afraid to branch out.

You can also use the search function to find people in your industry with whom you already have something in common. For example, you could try searching your college alumni page for people who work in your field. This gives you an "in" with people you might not otherwise connect with and allows you to cast a wider net while still keeping your search relevant. You should also consider joining groups that are specific to your interests and areas of expertise, where you can share your thoughts, interact with other members, and make new connections.

COVER LETTERS 101

While networking is by and large the most important job-hunting tool at your disposal, sooner or later, you'll find yourself facing the prospect of sitting down and writing a cover letter. If you're like most new job seekers, you'll probably have to send out more than one, and you probably won't get responses to many of the ones you do send out. And like most job seekers, I bet this will be the task you hate most. It's hard to write about yourself, and especially hard to do it in the engaging way required for a cover letter.

As you're going through this process, it's crucial not to get discouraged when you don't hear back from the companies you're cold calling. The trick is to keep sending out a steady stream of cover letters, starting with the positions you're most passionate about before moving on to the ones you care less strongly for.

While there's no way of guaranteeing a response, you can maximize your chances by writing a killer cover letter, and that means *not cutting any corners.* Job sites often include an "easy apply" option, where you only fill out your basic contact information and credentials without including a cover letter. This could be a big mistake. It's true some hiring managers don't read them. But others swear by them. Can you really take the chance? Cover letters are your friend, and a well-written cover letter really can be the difference between getting that critical interview and being passed over in favor of another candidate. Starting today, you need to learn to embrace cover letters and their ability to work in your favor.

So, what are the components of a well-written cover letter?

- **Brevity:** It's easy to get overly-wordy, especially when you're talking about yourself. Your rule of thumb should be not to let your letter run over a page. This may seem like a challenge at first but remember that you don't need to go into too much detail about what's already on your résumé. Instead, focus on what isn't obvious just from looking at your résumé.

- **Intent:** Remember: it's first and foremost about what you can do for others. This means you must include a statement of intent that focuses on how you plan to use your skills to contribute positively to the company and its goals.

- **Research:** I know. It's difficult to dig up information on every company you apply to, especially when there's no guarantee that you'll even hear back. But gathering information to leverage in your cover letter is invaluable, and it will also serve you well during your job interview.

  » Who is the hiring manager? Or if you can't find that, who would oversee the department to which you are applying?

  » What products and services does this company provide? How are these products and services relevant to you on a personal level?

  » You need to know a *lot* about the role you're applying for. Don't just skim the "qualifications" section of the listing and call it a day. Gather as much information as you can about what you'll be doing and who you'll be working with. Make sure your résumé speaks to the competencies the company is looking for. Consider using LinkedIn to find others at the company who have the same role. The more you know about the ins and outs of the job you want, the more specifically you can explain why you would be the perfect fit.

- **Polish:** Don't send anything out without proofreading it first. *Seriously.* The number of typos and grammar mistakes that make it past spell check are staggering. Equally important, especially when you're using a similar format for multiple letters: *Don't forget to change the name of the person you're sending it to whenever you write a new one!*

  Lack of polish is a one-way ticket to the rejection pile, which is why it's so important not to get sloppy. Take a break if you need to, rest your eyes if you need to, and make sure to have someone else review your letter before you send it.

- **Critical Thinking & Collaboration:** My friend, Brad Johnson, who you met in Chapter 2 really says it best: "Companies are looking for more than skills. They look for critical thinking skills and a collaborative team-oriented approach. They try to weed people out who don't do well in either of those. For the first, they will assess your skill in analyzing data with the case method. The latter is assessed more through subjective questioning." Your cover letter is a great opportunity to showcase both.

Remember, your cover letter *must* address why you are the perfect candidate for *this* job at *this* company. Write each one as if it's the only one you'll be sending out. This isn't the time to be modest.

Let's look at an example or two.

Example of a completely forgettable cover letter: (This is a fictional example, however it is representative of letters I see come in all the time.)

To whom it may concern,

I am writing to express my interest in the Virtual Assistant role at XYZ Company. I think this role would be a great opportunity to gain experience as an executive assistant in a professional setting.

Per my résumé, I am a recent graduate of ABC University with a bachelor's degree in Fine Art with a minor in business. I am a detail-oriented and a proficient multitasker. While I have never worked in a corporate setting, I am enthusiastic about this opportunity and ready to put my skills into practice at XYZ Company.

Thank you for your consideration, and I hope to hear from you soon.

Sincerely,

Johnny Appleseed

You'll notice that this cover letter is completely focused on the person applying and not on the company he's applying to. It is basically a restatement of his résumé that highlights the good opportunities for him but doesn't focus on how his skills will enhance the company.

While he has some unique qualifications, like his minor in business, he lists them the same way he would on a résumé. He doesn't go into any details about how he would use those qualifications to benefit the company, or what positive contributions he plans to make if he gets the job. Meanwhile, he draws attention to a negative aspect of his background, the fact that he's never worked in a corporate setting, instead of keeping the focus on his positive traits. There's no passion about the role, the organization, or even his own skills. It feels dry and formulaic, like he wrote one letter to use for all his applications and only changed the company name.

Would you hire him on the basis of that letter?

The next cover letter is a real example from our volunteer A.N. This one is better, but you'll see there is still a lot of room for improvement.

> *Dear Hiring Manager,*
>
> *Please accept my application for the Project Management Assistant position. I am a Junior at Babson College in Wellesley, MA and reside in Houston, TX. Beyond my role as a student at Babson, I serve as the Vice President of Membership for my sorority, Sigma Kappa Zeta Zeta, served as the President of Babson Hillel, and currently work as a Peer Mentor and a Foundations of Management and Entrepreneurship (FME) Mentor. I would love the opportunity to apply my accumulated skills in leadership, business, management, and collaboration to work toward Company XYZ's mission.*
>
> *Experiences I have accumulated since arriving at Babson and prior have prepared me to effectively meet expectations for the Project Management Internship. I gained experience in project management as the COO of my business during Babson's FME course, in which students create and run their own venture. I played a pivotal role in managing our team and business during the six-month life-span of our venture. After designing and conducting market research, I designed a product to appeal to our target market and established systems tracking sales and inventory and conceived creative methods of driving sales. I have since been working as an FME mentor for the past two years, influencing first year students as they have the opportunity to adopt the skills and thought processes of entrepreneurs. My most significant experience with project management is through my role as <u>Vice</u>*

President of Membership for my sorority. Throughout the academic year, my role requires me to plan recruitment events meant to expand our chapter's membership. I manage a calendar, maintain a budget, and oversee a committee during the course of planning events such as our formal recruitment or more small-scale events such as our table at the Babson College's Club and Org Fair. I have experience with and am confident using software such as Microsoft Project to organize and plan large scale projects.

Thank you for taking time to read and consider my application. I am eager to apply my knowledge of retail, supply chain management, and operations, and look forward to any opportunity to expand my business skills and experiences. I look forward to hearing from you and wish you well.

Best,

A.N

As you can see in this example, A.N. went into a lot more detail about her background. But it is basically a restatement of her résumé. There is still nothing about her passions—who *she* is as a person or what is important to her. There also is still a lack of how her skills will help the company. Now, Let's look at the final version:

Dear Ms. Smith,

As someone with a passion for operational organization and collaborative teambuilding and troubleshooting, I was thrilled to see that Company XYZ has an opening for a Project Management Assistant in the Human Resources department.

Having spent the last few years focused on studying strategic management and operational organization for my

Business Administration degree, I am particularly interested in working with Company XYZ because of your focus on effective and engaging management practices as well as your focus on providing educational programming for your employees. Your employees speak highly of your collaborative approach to project teams and development, and that is exactly the type of company for which I want to work. My past educational and work experience in event planning and operational management combined with my skills in creative solutioning and adaptability make me uniquely suited to being your Project Management Assistant.

I have long admired Company XYZ's commitment to promoting a positive workplace culture, and its impeccable reputation for diversity and inclusion, as well as its focus on giving back to the community—a personal priority for me. I am eager to use my energy and my experience in supply chain management, macro-level business operation analysis, and project management to contribute to that mission as your company seeks to expand to new markets.

Thank you very much for your time and consideration. I have included a copy of my résumé with this application. Please don't hesitate to reach out if you have any questions about my background or experience. I look forward to hearing from you.

Sincerely,
A.N.
123-456-7890
student@school.edu

Do you notice a difference?

In this cover letter, she took the time to find the name of the hiring manager instead of writing, "To whom it may concern," or "Dear Hiring Manager," which already makes it feel more personalized. She starts by expressing her enthusiasm about the open position and shows she has done research on the company's recent activities by commenting on their expansion to new markets and what employees have publicly said about the company. She also uses this as a chance to weave in relevant context about her qualifications that wouldn't be obvious from her résumé (her personal interest in community service) while emphasizing how her unique combination of skills would make her an asset to the company.

Finally, she wraps up the letter by expressing her gratitude to the hiring manager for taking the time to read her application and leaving the door open to further communication under the pretext of answering questions about her experience. You'll notice that she also includes her contact information at the bottom. This is always a good idea because it makes it easier for the hiring manager to get in touch with you.

The most important thing you can do in your cover letter is to frame your background as an asset, not to yourself, but to the company hiring you. They're the ones holding the cards right now, so playing to your skills is critical. It's a balance between putting your strong points on display and showing that you've done your homework. But if you can get it right, you'll set yourself apart from the dozens of applicants who don't bother to customize their cover letters.

COMPANY RED FLAGS

So far we've discussed how you have to tailor your application to the company. But there is another factor to consider. Do you really want to work for that company? When applying to jobs, you should also be researching them to see if the company aligns with your goals and your values. You may not find a company that meets every single expectation 100 percent of the time, so you have to decide where you are willing to compromise and where you are not. That is an entirely personal choice.

There are a lot of little clues that you can use to identify what a company is looking for, and what kind of culture they support. Remember, not every company culture is going to be a good fit for you. If there are issues that are really important to you, you need to see if the company is supportive or values the same thing. And you need to be looking for red flags that show a company's true colors.

This can be especially true for Diversity, Equity, & Inclusion (DE&I) applicants. According to Sophie Theen, an expert in Human Relations, if there is an internal employment diversity gap, the quickest and easiest way for a company to "solve" that problem is to hire someone new to fill that gap in a role or on a specific team. However, that doesn't mean they provide the level of support for those employees once they are in the company. You may not be able to discover this prior to applying, but you can add it to your list of questions to ask in your interview.

The first place to look is the job ad itself. Take a look at the language used. Are they using language like "kick-ass" or "hustlers." Or are they using language like "passionate" or "results-driven." This change in terminology can indicate that a company is trying to attract women to these positions. But if these are the only efforts a company makes, you could be in trouble down the road. This will come into play more later down the road, but for now it's important to be aware that just because a job post sounds like it would be a perfect fit doesn't mean the company can back that up in reality. But if you don't like the language used in the ad, respect that feeling. It won't get better, that much I can assure you.

Again, this is an opportunity to do some more research. If the ad sounds good, do other job ads on the company site mirror that language. Or is it just this position? Does the company showcase anything else that indicates its values? Now is the time to start learning that.

EMBRACING THE UNKNOWN.

This last section is really important for my favorite subject: mindset. I've said it before, and I'll say it again. Having the right mindset makes *all* the difference. During this process, you're going to face rejection. I bet you were expecting that. But what most people don't expect is the level of the unknown. You many not hear back immediately (or ever) from some jobs. Ghosting is a real problem for both applicants and businesses. It's long been an accepted practice for businesses to never respond to applicants. But that is starting to change primarily because applicants are ghosting them. It's a real problem for businesses. (And for future reference, don't be that person. If you aren't taking the job, buck up and just tell them. If you are quitting on day two, same thing. It's hard but it's the right thing to do.)[30] Remember that HR is a pretty small world. Again, think of your personal brand and professional identity.

The other important piece is don't get intimidated. Easier said than done, I know, especially when I've spent the last few chapters telling you what you should and shouldn't be doing. Seriously, though: the job search may be difficult, but it should never be frightening. If you let your anxiety about something build up in your mind, it will only get more intimidating, to the point where confronting it feels impossible. Your mindset is crucial: you can't be afraid of the unknown or of rejection.

Maybe your connections won't come through for you. You might not hear back from a hiring manager, or if you do, you might get nothing more than a formulaic, "thanks, but no thanks." It sucks, and I won't pretend it doesn't. It's scary and stressful putting yourself out there, especially when the odds are stacked against you. This is where reframing your thoughts comes in. Give yourself permission to fail. Better yet, see the process as a game. Every match you lose is practice for the next one, and every match you win is a step closer to the championship.

In the meantime, focus on what you *can* control. Make the search part of your daily life. Build the mindset into everything you do, from the places you go to the people you meet. Most importantly, *make connections.* Look for chances to meet people in relevant fields, and when you can't find any, start meeting people in fields that aren't relevant. Remember, that guy you give your information to that one time might just be the one who leads you to a killer job opening. Everyone you meet is a potential ally, and when you view other people as allies rather than enemies, the battle becomes a lot less intimidating. In short: opportunity is everywhere if you know where to look.

#PACE PROCESS STEPS

- **Be prepared for "Hybrid" questions.** The world is changing. Be prepared to answer questions about how you will manage working in a hybrid or remote space.
- **Research, research, research!** I'm pretty sure you hate that word by this point, but you shouldn't. It should become a lifestyle. It will serve you well in everything you do, from applying for a job, to working, to home repairs.

- **Reframe your experience into something useful.** Think how skills apply to different situations. Use active verbs. Showcase accomplishments and specific data-driven results.
- **Commit to writing custom cover letters for each job.** This can't be skipped. No copy-and-paste letters.
- **Maintain a strong mindset.** Don't let a little rejection get you down. It only makes you stronger! The perfect job is out there. Just keep networking.

CHAPTER 5

INTERVIEWING SUCCESS

YOU'VE DONE IT! You've hustled your heart out, you've sent out applications, and you've made a concerted effort to find opportunities within your network … and it's paid off! You've gotten that callback, you've scored that interview, and you're well on your way. But now is not the time to get complacent. Getting that first bite is only half the battle.

It's important to remember that landing an interview doesn't mean you're in. It means you've passed the first hurdle, and that's a worthy accomplishment. But you can't assume it's all just going to work out from here on. You may have several interviews ahead for a single position. Typically, three interviews are pretty standard, but I've heard of companies doing five or more! You need to look at the long game and prepare accordingly. Given the new realities of hybrid work, we are going to cover some traditional tips for interviews as well as some added tips for Zoom interviews. There is a lot of crossover, but Zoom interviews present a unique set of challenges. These will also be tips that can carry over into the hybrid space once you have the job.

BUILDING YOUR PERSONAL BRAND

This is going to sound awfully corporate, but since we're talking about the corporate world, it makes sense. Whether you like it or not, career success is all about sales. The only difference is that instead of selling a product, *you're selling yourself.* We've talked some already about building your brand, but we are going to go into a bit more detail here.

Ask yourself this: *would I buy something if the person selling it doesn't know what it does or how it can benefit me?* Probably not, right? Interviews are your chance to promote yourself, which means that if you're savvy, you'll use them wisely. That means having an intimate understanding of who you are, what you're good at, what you're looking for, and most importantly, *what sets you apart from everyone else.* This is your personal brand.

IDENTIFYING YOUR NICHE

"Niche" is a word you have probably heard buzzing around. It gets tossed around in corporate circles all the time, and for good reason. Having a niche gives you value. It makes you more appealing for positions in the area in which you are best. It helps you create a targeted plan of action that will propel you throughout your career, and it's something you can fall back on whenever you feel you're losing momentum.

There's this myth that having a niche will make you less employable or give you less access to a broad range of jobs. I'm here to tell you that this is 100 percent wrong. The thing about a niche is that it's a subcategory of a broader area of expertise. For example, content writing is a subcategory of marketing. Focusing on content writing doesn't lock you out of all other marketing jobs; in fact, you have to be a capable marketer in order to become an effective content writer in the first place. Just like a lawyer needs a working knowledge of the law in general in order to focus on, let's say, civil rights law. You need a working knowledge of your overall field in order to focus on your chosen niche. Finding a niche doesn't limit your opportunities. It gives you a targeted specialization that you can pursue while continuing to learn about the umbrella it falls under.

Questions to ask yourself when finding your niche:

- **What am I passionate about?** This is where you always want to start. Jot down a list of things you enjoy and find interesting. What are your hobbies? What do you enjoy doing and *look forward* to doing when you're not working? Don't be afraid to think outside the box. What websites or types of articles do you browse in your spare time? What kinds of books and magazines do you read? What excites you?

- **What am I good at?** Take a step back and think about your strengths. In previous jobs and internships, what earned you the most praise? Consider asking people you know—friends, family, former supervisors, and former teachers—what they think your best skills and traits are. Getting outside opinions is a great way to keep your thinking objective.

- **What problem can I solve with this?** This is a great question for entrepreneurs, but it's also worth asking yourself if you're stuck and can't figure out how to capitalize on your skills. If something can be marketed, then there's most likely a job to be found that's related to it. If your interests are a little more "out there," then you may have a harder time finding an interesting role right out of the gate, but that doesn't mean you shouldn't look. *As a side note, this is another great reason to keep expanding your network. You never know what interesting things might pop up.*

Now that you've considered these questions, tie them back to your career. How do these things tie into the job you are applying for, or the company itself?

Keep in mind that now is the time for objectivity. If you've always loved photography but you've never excelled at it or had any formal training, it might be a better idea to keep it as a hobby, at least for now. Maybe you can get a job that's still tangentially related, like at a gallery, while you build up your skills. What you're going for is a balance between what's interesting and what's feasible.

ESTABLISHING YOUR STORY

Everyone has a story. It's a part of being human, and it's one of your best tools for getting your career off the ground. People love stories. They remember stories. Your story sets you apart from everyone else, because no two people arrived where they are in exactly the same way. When you think of Tom Brady, what comes to mind? How he overcame adversity? How he works harder than anyone? How he motivates himself by acknowledging that he was a sixth-round draft pick (#199)?

Now's your chance to think about your background outside of what you would put on your résumé. Where were you born? What was your childhood like? How did you develop your interests? Do you have any memories that really helped solidify the person that you are? Audrey Hepburn came of age during the Dutch famine of World War II. Howard Schultz grew up poor in the projects of Brooklyn. Bill Gates wrote his first software program when he was thirteen.

When I think about my formative years, what always jumps out at me is the memory of being surrounded by hard-working people. The neighborhoods where I grew up were solidly blue-collar, gritty, and rough around the edges, but the people there were incredibly dedicated to their jobs. Hard work was built into the spirit of the community. Looking back, it was almost inevitable that I developed an entrepreneurial spirit. Through watching the people around me and working odd jobs around town, I learned that I could make money while doing things that made people happy—things that were motivating, inspiring, and fun. Through navigating my own career, I've arrived at my philosophy of passing success, knowledge, and positive experiences on to other people.

This is a bite-sized account of what drives me as a businessman, and how my story has made me into the person I am today. As you write your own story, consider what motivates, inspires, and interests you. If you were writing your own biography, what events would you include? Try thinking about the stories of people you look up to and looking for the ways they mirror your own.

Remember, when someone asks you about yourself, you're not giving them your full autobiography. Focus on the key parts that will make yourself memorable, interesting, and dynamic. Find your personal spark and use it to impress your potential employer. Your story will be an intriguing blurb, something you'll always have in your back pocket to spice up conversations and leave a strong impression on the people you connect with.

Going back to my friend, Brad Johnson, he has a great example. He has interviewed thousands of people over the years, and the sad thing is that most of them have very cookie-cutter answers. To stand out, try to come up with some memorable examples that address analytical skills and some that showcase your teamwork. These also don't have to be work examples. Get creative. Examples from internships, sports teams, school, or even your personal passions work as well, especially when you're just getting started.

Here's a great example Brad provided from his experience.

"One applicant had something on his résumé about how his goal was to watch the 500 best movies of all time. It was just small talk at the time, but I still remember asking him how he knew they were the top 500. He told me all about the movie database IMDb.com. As he's chatting, he casually mentions that he engineered his own algorithm based on that data to apply to TV shows as well so that he could also watch the top 500 TV shows of all time. All I could think was, 'Yeah, this is the guy I want on my team.'"

The job this man was applying for had nothing to do with the entertainment industry, but it did have a lot to do with data analysis, algorithms, and statistics. His passion covered all those topics and Brad barely had to ask him anything to find that out. This just goes to show you how a seemingly non-relevant example can you get you the job!

SELLING YOURSELF

As I said earlier, getting a job is all about selling yourself, which means interviewing for a job is like making a sales pitch. Your skills, background, and experience are all important factors, but *how* you present these things is equally important. From the minute you walk in the door, everything about you—from how you dress to how you speak—is being observed. The interviewer is forming opinions and making judgments based on your entire presence, and not what's written on your résumé. Remember, whether or not you're a good fit for a job is based on more than your résumé; it's based on the energy you give off, and how well you'll synergize with other people at the company. Job interviews are intimidating, but they're also your chance to make a case for yourself. Who are you? What's your story? What's your niche? These are all questions to ask yourself as you prepare. Distilling your most important qualities into an image and developing your personal brand are the biggest tools in your toolbox.

It seems obvious, but you would be surprised how many people forget the simple point of *making a killer first impression.* This is more important than you realize. Our brains can handle forty pieces of information consciously, but subconsciously that number is *11 million!*[31] That means that the information our brain collects in seconds can impact our perception of those around us. In any situation, professional or not, other people's first impression of you colors how they view you from there on out. Here are some things to consider:

- **Eye contact.** The best way to let someone know you're interested in what they're saying is by looking at them as they speak. The same goes for when you're the one speaking; if you're staring down at your lap as you give an answer, you come across as evasive and unsure of yourself. Eye contact projects confidence and engagement as long as it projects genuine interest and doesn't look like staring. Try to follow the 50/70 rule: look someone in the eyes 50 percent of the time while talking, and 70 percent of the time while listening.

  » **Zoom Tip:** In this new hybrid workplace, many interviews are now being conducted by Zoom. It can be hard to connect with your interviewer this way. Try positioning their image in Zoom in a small window at the top-center of your screen, directly beneath the camera lens. This will give the appearance that you are looking directly at your interviewer and making eye contact, whereas placing their image in a bottom corner makes you look down and veils your eyes. This can make is appear as if you're not paying attention, (even when you are).

- **Hygiene.** It's embarrassing to talk about, but it needs to be said: bad hygiene can be very off-putting, especially in a professional context. Shower, brush your teeth, trim your nails. Don't be afraid to ask someone you know to evaluate your hygiene. It's always better to have someone you trust point out the food in your teeth than to realize it on your way out of the interview.
  - » **Zoom Tip:** You might think this can be skipped in a Zoom call. However, that's a bad idea. You can still have food stuck in your teeth, greasy hair or other issues that will be noticeable on screen. And you'd be surprised how many people still talk with their hands on video calls. Every aspect of your appearance should be neat and tidy. Especially since, if you are doing a group interview, they may have your image up on the big screen in the office!

- **Speaking clearly.** Mumbling is a no-go. It's like avoiding eye contact, in that it makes you seem insecure and self-conscious. *Don't be afraid to slow down.* I can't emphasize this enough. We tend to assume people expect us to speak quickly, but there's no need for it. Taking a breath, collecting your thoughts, and choosing what you want to say carefully before you say it helps you sound professional. It shows the interviewer that you're someone who thinks things through before you speak, which is always a positive trait. Since nervousness makes us talk more quickly, slowing down makes you appear more composed. The person you're speaking to has set this time aside specifically to talk to you, so there's no need to rush through what you're saying!

» **Zoom Tip:** Make sure you test your microphone beforehand. Consider wearing a Bluetooth headset, preferably one that is small and nearly hidden in your ear. You will be able to hear them clearly without distractions and they will be able to hear you clearly as well.

- **Practice social self-awareness.** In job interviews, in *any* conversation, for that matter, it's crucial to be mindful of how you're being perceived. The best way to do this is to put yourself in the interviewer's shoes. Try to see yourself from their perspective. If you were the one asking the questions, what would you want to see? Would you look for someone cocky and arrogant, or gracious and mindful? Listen to what the interviewer is saying, instead of just waiting for your turn to speak. Don't interrupt. If you have conflicting views, try to find a middle ground. Even if you're getting bad vibes, or *they're* the one giving you a bad impression, be courteous. The higher road will take you a long way.

  » **Zoom Tip:** Interrupting can be a bit of an issue on video calls. If there is any type of lag in the signal, you may unintentionally interrupt, or someone may interrupt you. Be graceful in such situations. Don't be afraid to take a pause before answering a question. It can even make you appear thoughtful!

- **Smile, damn it!** It's worth giving a genuine smile here and there. I don't mean in a creepy way—so don't take this as an invitation to sit there and grin the whole time—but being overly-serious can be a turn-off. Smiling automatically diffuses some of the tension in a situation, and gives the vibe that you're, well, happy to be there. Makes sense, right?

» **Zoom Tip:** Smile, damn it!
- **Executive presence.** Now that you've begun cultivating your personal brand, you need to figure out how to present it. Think of yourself as your own CEO. How will you act? How will you talk? What posture will you adopt?
  - » **Zoom Tip:** This still holds true. Posture, in particular, can be very evident on a Zoom call. But beyond that, your surroundings make an impact as well. Pick your spot with intention. Find a tidy, professional place to hold your interview. If that is not possible, utilize Zoom backgrounds to hide the chaos behind you. Just make sure you select a professional one. "Under The Sea" may be fun, but it's not appropriate for a job interview.
- **Dress to impress.** Of course, this will depend on where you're trying to land a job. Aim for slightly dressier than is strictly necessary.
  - » **Zoom Tip:** As with executive presence, this also holds true for Zoom interviews. And to avoid embarrassing accidents, As a side note, *wear pants*. Now that I think about it, wear pants for any video call, interview or not (even though they don't show on camera.) Be professional from head to toe. Not only will it help you avoid any mishaps, being dressed to impress is like wearing armor. It helps you feel prepared and ready for what is to come. It can give you the psychological boost you need to make that killer first impression.
- **Be on time.** Don't forget to set your alarm, knucklehead! Aim for arriving at your interview fifteen minutes early. This gives you extra time to prepare and gives you a buffer in case you run into trouble getting there. Most importantly,

though, it shows the interviewer that you're prepared and eager.

> » **Zoom Tip:** Most hiring managers have mastered this process, but a few still seem to use the same link for all interviews. If you get on a call too early, you could be interrupting them. Not that you would be able to join the call without their permission, but it would pop up on their screen. Be mindful of their time and try to join your interview no more than five minutes early.

- **Build confidence.** Okay, so maybe this isn't something you can just do overnight. I get it. Some people are more extroverted than others. The thing is, if you're not confident, it shows. Have faith in your brand, and the experience and knowledge you bring to the table. You've spent time identifying your strengths and figuring out how they apply to the job you have in mind. You've earned the right to be confident! You wouldn't have been called in for an interview otherwise!

  The best way to grow confidence is to fake it 'til you make it, so change your mindset to "this will be a no-brainer." Optimism will go far here. When the interviewer asks about your weaknesses, frame them in the context of your strengths. For example, instead of saying, "I'm disorganized and I'm bad at math and science," you could say, "My biggest strength is that I'm such a creative person, so I tend to lean more toward intuition and the arts than logic and linear thinking."

  > » **Zoom Tip:** Confidence can be harder to convey over Zoom. This really relies on the tips I gave above. Carry yourself well—have good posture. Try to imitate

making eye contact. Speak clearly and assuredly. Have a professional presentation. When in doubt, there are a lot of resources for building confidence online.[32]

- **Practice what you believe in.** In other words, put your money where your mouth is. It's not enough just to want something and skate by on your degree. If you want to become a professional chef, you should be practicing cooking at home. If you want to become a bestselling novelist, you should be writing at home. The same goes for any corporate job. Stay up to date on trends, technologies, and the direction the market is going. Your studies aren't over just because you're done with school. Research—it's a lifestyle.

  » **Zoom Tip:** Zoom is actually an advantage here. You can have notes and your interviewer will never know! However, if you're looking down too often and clearly reading from notes, it will be a giveaway. Write down the most important points and questions you have on sticky notes and place them around your screen. No looking down necessary!

- **What can I do for you?** The key to a successful job interview is the same as the key to successful networking: to prove that you are both invaluable and one-of-a-kind. Remember how you researched the company before writing your cover letter? It's time for that information to come back into play. Don't be afraid to get creative with this. What is the company's corporate culture like? What are its strengths and how do they overlap with yours? Discuss your experience doing similar work. If this is your first real job, your experience doesn't have to be exactly the same, so think about broader experiences that apply to this role. For example, if you're applying to a public relations job, think of times you've had to plan or organize events, conduct research, use written communication, etc.

An important exercise to prepare for your interview is to put yourself in the shoes of the interviewer. If you really want to make yourself stand out, research the person you will be meeting with ahead of time using information from their company website or LinkedIn page. If any fun or interesting information jumps out at you, use it as an icebreaker. Remember, this isn't about you. It's about what the company needs. Think about this from the perspective of the hiring manager: If you were them, what would you be looking for in a candidate? This is the same process you went through when you wrote your cover letter.

That said, you are also interviewing the company. You are looking for clues that you want to work for the company and be a part of their team. Remember, you're also looking for red flags that may indicate it is not the place for you. In most interviews, they will give you an opportunity to ask any questions you have. You should always have at least one question prepared. They will expect it, and not having one can make it appear that you aren't doing your due diligence, or that you are not serious about the position. It can come across like you just don't care. So what should you ask?

There are a lot of options here. You could go with the classics:

- What benefit package do you offer?
- What's a typical day or schedule look like?
- Do you offer flexible hours?
- Do you have a specific promotion schedule?

There are also some questions that you can use to identify red flags, values, or other information about the company.

- What is the company culture like?
- Do you offer mentorship resources or support resources to new employees?
- What is your DE&I policy
- What are your policies for working remotely from international locations?
- What is your favorite thing about working for this company?

Some of these questions may be answered in the interview naturally, without you having to ask. That's why it is important to have some backup questions ready just in case.

SUBJECT MATTER EXPERTISE

This is also a good time to consider your story and your unique set of skills. How does your background make you a unique fit for this role? What skills do you have that may be an unexpected asset? Most candidates for a position are going to have the same basic set of skills. For example, if you're interviewing for a software engineering position, your competition will likely have similar skills and experience in coding. You still need to make your expertise in those skills evident, but you also want to showcase anything else that you can add to the position and company?

Let's look at an example. A young woman I know applied for a job at a tech company. The job required skills in marketing, copywriting, SEO, and technical writing. However, during the interview process she went in prepared with ideas on how to systemize aspects of the department in which she'd be working—aspects they hadn't even considered yet as needing systemization. She also went on to tell them how she was teaching herself basic coding and design skills—both of which would be useful to expedite pieces of her job without relying on other employees and taking them away from bigger projects. She got the job!

WHAT HIRING MANAGERS ARE LOOKING FOR

We've touched on a few things hiring managers are looking for: specific skill sets for the job, the company's needs, and a professional, team-oriented attitude. After talking with several industry professionals and HR experts, we've compiled a list of questions that my contacts love to ask. You can rest assured that other hiring managers will be looking for similar things.

First: a proven track record. Show that you have handled similar projects with a specific set of results your employer can count on. You've likely highlighted this on your résumé, but the interview is your opportunity to really showcase your successes.

Many companies also require an assessment test of your skills. Scoring well on these assessments helps… but it also isn't everything. Don't give up just because you didn't do as well as you thought. Instead, reframe that score with additional context. A colleague of mine from early in my career has the perfect example, but for privacy reasons, they have contributed this anonymously "We had an individual we wanted to hire for a big job. But we had some reservations after the assessment. He didn't score as well as we wanted on the assessment, yet his references were stellar. We were missing something, and I didn't feel like I was getting great answers. I went back to one of them and asked for more information as to why he had recommended the applicant so strongly. The reference understood the dilemma. He said, 'This applicant is the type to execute very efficiently, not strategize. He doesn't plan, he executes.' We hired him because that was exactly what we needed in this position." In this situation, his assessment was less important given the context of his other skills.

Interviewers will also ask some out-of-left-field questions. They are listening not only for the answer but also your thought process. They want to know you are reflective, accountable, humble, self-aware, and more. Taking a moment to really consider your answer to the question is totally appropriate. Take that time. Here are a few examples:

- Tell me a story about something that you were personally responsible for that went sideways. What did you learn? What would you do differently?
- What have you learned recently that's new, and how did you learn it?
- Give me an example of a great success in your life. Even with all that success, is there anything you would do differently?
- Tell me a story about someone who impacted your life personally or professionally. When have you done that for someone else?
- Give me an example of a decision you made. What was your process for making that decision?
- Describe a time when you were able to convince a leader to adopt your point of view.
- Tell me a story about a time when you had to make a decision in the absence of complete data.
- Describe a situation when you had a conflict with a colleague. How did you resolve it?
- Tell me about the role you are interviewing for today.
- Do you already see any core priorities that you want to dig into?
- Tell me about the last gift you gave someone.

These are just a few examples. You can't prepare for every eventuality, so the best advice I can give you hear is to stay calm, take a moment to think, and be creative. Take the fourth question above about making decisions. This doesn't have to be a professional decision. If you have a good example of a personal decision that had similarly high stakes, use it! They are looking for the process, the outcome, and what you learned from making that decision. They won't really care about the specific details of the decision itself. Just remember—don't get flustered. Remain professional, sincere, and honest at all times. I respect people more who have the courage to say "I don't know, but I'll get back to you on that" than those who clearly are making up weak examples.

GETTING OUTSIDE PERSPECTIVE.

No one knows exactly how an interview will go down. There may be curveballs, questions you aren't prepared for, or remarks that throw you for a loop. That's why it's important not to go in blind. The best thing you can do to prepare is to practice. Think of it as doing a favor to your future self.

I would recommend enlisting someone to help you. This could be a friend, a professor, a parent, and so on, even an outside mentor. (We'll discuss mentors further in Chapter 7.) This must be someone you trust to give you honest and constructive feedback. Have them conduct a mock interview and don't let them go easy on you. Research common interview questions and figure out your responses. Practice posture, eye contact, and pacing. Afterward, ask for their honest opinion on how you did. Now is not the time to hold back!

Consider recording yourself during these practice sessions as well. Replay the video after you've received your feedback and have them point out everything they noticed. Were you mumbling without realizing? Did you seem tense or uncomfortable? Did you say "um" a lot? Seeing yourself after the fact will give you an objective view of your performance, and help you pinpoint exactly what you need to work on. You can't practice too much. You may not be in your comfort zone, but every time you go over what you're going to say and how you're going to act, you're that much more prepared for when the time comes.

This advice also applies to your résumé and cover letter, too. Getting a second, (or even third or fourth) opinion can be immensely valuable. You can even take someone with you to go shopping for the perfect outfit for your interview. And on that note, you don't have to go with haute couture, or expensive brands. If your resources are limited, don't go crazy. It could even come from the thrift store. Just look for something clean, professional, and well-fitting. That will make the right first impression.

FOLLOWING THROUGH

When all is said and done and you're leaving the interview, it's tempting to try to forget about it and hope for the best. Don't. Your job isn't done yet, and if you want to make a lasting impression, you still have work to do.

Following up with your interviewer reinforces your interest in the position. If done correctly, it also demonstrates that you were paying attention during your conversation, took to heart the most important parts, and are able to address them succinctly. An email is a great way to go, but in some cases a hand-written note can be appropriate as well. Start by thanking them again for taking the time to meet you. Follow this with an affirmation of how much you'd love the chance to work at this particular company. Make sure to reference a specific point from your conversation (as an example, bring up something that interests you, how you feel connected to something related to one of the company's goals, or an aspect of the corporate culture that you think is important for the company to thrive) and find a way to tie it to your aspirations, skills, and background. Finish up with a brief statement on what sets you apart from other candidates, along with your contact information.

If you feel you made a mistake during the interview, mention this in your follow-up email. Be sure to only address issues you're sure were obvious to the interviewer, otherwise you risk drawing their attention to a problem they wouldn't have otherwise noticed. Don't make excuses. For example, express your regret that you misinterpreted a question or didn't explain yourself clearly, and then reiterate your passion and enthusiasm about the job. This is also a chance to give them any important information you forgot to mention during your conversation, whether work experience or background information.

Follow-up messages can lead to a starting position. Even a simple message thanking them for their time will go a long way. Most people don't send anything at all! But best practices call for something like this:

Follow-up email example:

> *Dear Ms. Smith,*
>
> *Thank you again for taking the time to meet with me today to discuss the Project Management Assistant position. It was an absolute pleasure to speak with you and learn more about this role, your team, and your company. I am thrilled about the prospect of joining Company XYZ and the HR team, and I was very interested to hear about your company's plans to expand employee programming events. Given my previous experience in event planning and coordination, I'm excited I can contribute to this expansion in meaningful ways.*

> *Please let me know if you have any further questions,*
> *or if you need anything further from me. I look forward to*
> *hearing from you.*
> *Sincerely,*
> *A.N.*

There may come a time when you need to send a second follow-up email. Perhaps they said they would notify you by a specific date, and that date has come and gone. While you might want to give them an extra day, just in case, it would be appropriate to follow up after that. Here is a good example of that email.

Follow-up email example 2:

> *Dear Ms. Smith,*
> *It was wonderful speaking with you on Monday about*
> *the role of Project Management Assistant. I just wanted to*
> *follow up with you again about the position and see if you*
> *had any further questions. You mentioned that you were*
> *looking to fill the role immediately and I want to reiterate*
> *my interest and passion for this role and your company. I look*
> *forward to hearing from you soon.*
> *Sincerely,*
> *A.N.*

#PACE PROCESS STEPS

- **Identify your brand and your specialization.** Figure out where your interests and your skills intersect with the company and position for which you are applying. Use this information to help you prepare for your interview. Think back on formative events in your life to create a story that's uniquely yours.

- **Sell yourself and bring 110 percent to your interview.** Go beyond the basics, like hygiene and dressing well. Be on time, make eye contact, speak clearly and at a clear pace. Project an air of confidence (even if you don't actually feel confident). Remember your *executive presence*. If you're interviewing by Zoom, make sure to review the Zoom tips.
- **Ask for feedback from others.** Practice, practice, practice. Find someone who can give you a mock interview without avoiding the hard questions. Prepare answers for common interview questions, as well as the "out-of-left-field" questions. Record yourself, so you can watch it again later and understand how others perceive you. Get feedback on your presence, charisma, and responses. The more you go over this, the easier it will be when you actually walk into the interview room, or connect on a Zoom call.
- **Prepare your questions for *them*.** You'll want some backups just in case the more obvious ones are answered in the interview itself. Having a thoughtful question prepared will also give them insight into you and your values.
- **Follow up.** Reach out to everyone who interviews you. Thank them for their time and call their attention back to key parts of your conversation. Remind them of your interest in the job and reiterate why you think it would be a good fit for you. If you want to address anything else that happened during the interview, this is your chance.

CHAPTER 6

HANDLING UNCERTAINTY AND FAILURE

AT SOME POINT DURING YOUR CAREER DOUBTS will start creeping in. You'll catch yourself wondering whether you're pursuing the right job, whether you're making the right moves, whether your strategy is the right one. This happens a lot when you're just starting your career, and that's understandable. In the beginning, you're still calibrating your approach to work in general. But these doubts do not stop the minute you get your first job; many times, they amplify. There will be moments over the course of your career when you start asking yourself those questions, and if you're not careful, you'll end up spinning out of control. The issue isn't that you're reflecting on where you are—introspection is always a good thing—but that when you start letting doubts control the narrative, your mindset can become self-defeating.

That's why it's crucial to address these doubts before they take hold and develop your strategy for handling them when they do. The Apply stage is when this really will start. Like I said, it doesn't go away, but this is your first opportunity to start learning how to deal with it and learning to develop coping mechanisms.

SILENCING YOUR INNER CRITIC

There's a little voice inside all of us that's constantly feeding us negatives. It's common—so common, in fact, that psychologists have actually given it a name. They call it the inner critic, and it's a near-universal human trait. It's the side of us that tells us we're ugly whenever we look in the mirror, that calls us a failure whenever we make mistakes, that insists we should just give up now and stop trying. The inner voice feeds on our fears, insecurities, past experiences, and constantly tells us that we're not good enough. It makes us question our decisions and amplifies our flaws; it can take control of our lives if we let it.

You'll probably start hearing from your inner critic a lot. Most people do, including me. "Look at you," it might say. "Do you really think you can do this? You have no experience, you're too timid, all the other applicants are better than you. You're naive to think you even have a shot at this job." Sometimes it rears its ugly head after you've gotten your foot in the door. "You shouldn't have gotten this job," it might try to tell you. "You have no idea what you're doing here. You're not worthy of this job or promotion, and sooner or later everyone will realize it."

Pretty gut wrenching, right? That voice will say anything to shake your sense of self-worth, whether you're on the hunt for a job or on your way to a promotion. But if you let those doubts control you, you will end up selling yourself short. So how do we tell that inner critic to shut up?

COUNTERING NEGATIVE THOUGHTS

The thing about the inner critic is that it always talks in black and white. There's no room for mistakes, and there's no middle ground. I'm here to tell you that that's complete BS. The real world is almost never black and white, and reminding yourself of this can keep you from spinning out. To counter these negative thoughts, practice turning your doubts into something more constructive. For example:

- **Negative:** I'm terrible at talking to people and networking. No one will want to connect with me.
- **Constructive:** Even though it's stressful, if I pretend to have confidence it will become real to those around me. I just need to take it one conversation, one connection at a time.
- **Negative:** I don't have enough experience for this role. I'm never going to get it.
- **Constructive:** My résumé is light in some areas, but my skills and work ethic are strong. I'll have to really sell myself, but I still have a shot.
- **Negative:** I got the job, but the hiring manager must have made a mistake. I'll never be able to do it.
- **Constructive:** The hiring manager wouldn't have hired me if they didn't see something in me. I don't have to be an expert going in, as long as I'm willing to roll up my sleeves and learn.

Taking a step back and changing the tone of your doubts helps you put them in a context that's less self-defeating and more realistic.

FOCUSING ON YOUR ACCOMPLISHMENTS

This is another strategy for countering self-doubt as it arises. Sometimes we don't struggle with a specific issue, but instead find ourselves questioning everything without considering all the great things we've done. We'll wonder if we've been on the wrong path this whole time, and doubt that we're worthy of our successes even when they do happen. A great technique to counter this is to put your attention on your victories and not your losses.

Make a list of accomplishments that have really given you a boost in the past. These could be anything from nailing a final exam to getting great feedback on a project. They don't have to be related to your career path. Just focus on moments in the past, big or small, that made you feel good about your abilities. Whenever something else positive happens, you can add it to the list. Every time you catch yourself getting caught up in self-doubt, return to those accomplishments as a reminder that you're more capable than you think.

ALLOWING FOR THE POSSIBILITY THAT YOU'RE WRONG

It's simple, but it can sometimes be all you need to get yourself back on track. The thing about self-doubt is that when we question ourselves, we tend to assume that the negative things we tell ourselves are correct. This goes back to a black and white mentality, and this false idea that if we're having doubts in the first place, there must be something wrong with us.

But what if those thoughts are totally untrue?

Practice doubting your doubts. Here are some examples.

- **Doubt:** I don't think I'm cut out for this career path.
- **Response:** I won't know unless I give it a shot. It might be the perfect fit.
- **Doubt:** Nobody else in my role is struggling as much I am. I must be doing something wrong.

- **Response:** For all I know, everyone else in my role is having these same doubts. I might not be as alone as I think I am. All I have to do is do the best I can in this moment.

It's possible that your doubts are coming from an irrational place, so stop taking them as fact. Uncertainty is part of being human, and more often than not, we're our own worst critics. Allow yourself room to make mistakes, especially when it comes to assumptions you make about yourself and your abilities.

TAKING CONTROL OF WHAT YOU CAN CHANGE

What can I do now? Not tomorrow, not next year, but now? We can't predict the future, and we can't have complete control over things that haven't happened yet. Isn't it funny we tend to panic the most when we're thinking about what lies months and years in front of us?

You would be surprised how empowering it is to just take control of what's immediately accessible to you. When uncertainty strikes, stop playing the long game and concentrate on what you can do *right now*. Can you send an email to your mentor asking for their advice? Can you revise your résumé? Can you research entry-level opportunities? Great. Do it! Then repeat the process again tomorrow. And the day after that. Don't let yourself get wrapped up in thinking about how you'll get from a job you don't have yet to a job you want five years from now. This, too, is important, but it can be counterproductive when you're struggling with the uncertainty of the future. Take a breath, take stock of what productive things you can do now, and focus on those.

Just start. Once you've figured out what you can tackle from where you are right now, all there is to do is get started. I've said it before, and I'll say it again, because it bears repeating: the inertia of getting started is *the hardest part* of any big accomplishment. Once you get momentum going, the process becomes easier the longer you work at it. Overcoming this initial hump is even harder when you're in an uncertain situation, and you may find yourself wondering if it's worth trying, since the results may not be what you hoped for. This comes from faulty perfectionist thinking—why bother trying if it won't be perfect out the gate? Don't fall into this trap. Even if it doesn't turn out perfect—and it sometimes won't—that doesn't mean it's not worth pursuing.

Stop half-assing it. This goes hand-in-hand with my last point. As difficult as it is to muster motivation when you're doubting yourself, remember this: a small task done well is worth ten times more than a big task done poorly. So instead of biting off more than you can chew, getting burned out, and doing a sloppy job, focus on doing the absolute best you can on what you believe you can successfully manage at one time. Send out one perfect application instead of five that are half-baked. Go to one networking event and give it your all instead of going to three and being a wallflower. Ask your boss what their top priority item is and put your full attention on it. Sometimes all it takes to perform better is targeted effort instead of scattered motivation.

… and accepting what you can't change.

Change the narrative. By now you've probably gathered that I'm big on reframing thoughts and experiences. That's because even when we can't change our situation, we can decide how we react to it and how we contextualize it. Think about how you reframe negative thoughts in a constructive light and do the same thing for overall uncertainty. Instead of viewing the job search as an intimidating hurdle, view it as an adventure, complete with the ups, downs, and rewards that come with any sort of meaningful journey. Launching your career is a right of passage. You don't have to have it all figured out right now, so instead of fighting the chaos, embrace it.

- **Plan ahead.** If you're someone with more perfectionist tendencies, it can help to have a plan for when things don't go your way. Even if you can't foresee everything, you can at least have some sense of security as you navigate the unknown.

- **Create your safety net.** Building an emergency fund is always a good idea. This isn't always possible, but you should do your best to have some money on hand in case things don't work out. If getting a job takes longer than you expected, or if you *do* get a job and it doesn't work out, you'll have some wiggle room to find a better opportunity. Maintain a community you can turn to if things don't go your way and make practical preparations for the worst-case scenario. As motivational speaker Denis Waitley says, "Expect the best, plan for the worst, and prepare to be surprised."[33]

- **Keep your feelers out.** When the future is uncertain—even when things are going well—keeping your eyes peeled for new opportunities is the best favor you can do for yourself. Don't let your network stagnate just because you've gotten a good job or your prospects are looking good. Reach out to your connections periodically, even if it is just to say hello. And if appropriate, you can tell them that you're on the lookout for new projects and remember the golden question: "What can *I* do for *you?*" Holiday cards (or emails) can also be a great way to maintain a connection. It's old school, but effective!

- **Maintain your skills, especially the ones you're not currently using.** There are a few abilities that nearly every employer looks for in their hires. Writing and communication. Frustration tolerance. The ability to interpret data. Curiosity. Problem-solving and the ability to get to the root of an issue. Organization and analysis. Just because you're done with school, that doesn't mean you have a free pass to let your skills get rusty. Read up on building a learning mindset, interpreting information, and effectively communicating.

  I'm a big believer in reading. There are a lot of great books out there than can provide useful tools, skills, or mindsets. But even if you're reading about topics unrelated to your work, reading keeps your mind engaged and primed for learning. Even reading for just thirty minutes each day means you will read thirty-three books *each year!*[34] Find a system that works for you—alternate fiction with nonfiction, or narrative with educational, or work-related with fun.

  You can also practice the skills and specializations that you aren't using in your current situation, and don't be afraid to think outside the box. Whether you commit an hour a day after work or a couple hours on the weekend, the time you spend will greatly benefit you in the long run. Have you been concentrating on the humanities, but always wanted to learn to code? Consider making it your new hobby. Have you wanted to improve your writing abilities? Try starting a blog, even if no one reads it. At worst, you have something extra to add to your CV, and at best, you're opening the door to brand new opportunities.

Doubts and uncertainty affect all of us, often at unexpected times, but we can't take it to heart. By reframing our worries and insecurities, we can retake control of the narrative without letting it cripple us. We are in command of our individual success or of our destinies, if you prefer that outlook. Reframing your mindset should be a daily goal, and as you get better at it, it will get easier and easier.

You may not be able to change everything, but by changing what you can, you are reinforcing your ability to cope with the unknown instead of fearing it. Building these skills now will take you far in your career, even when the landscape is rocky.

> *"Success consists of going from failure to failure without loss of enthusiasm."*
> —Winston Churchill

Here's a not-so-nice truth about the reality of work: you're going to fail, and if you're like most people, you're going to fail a lot. Many people don't know—or have never learned—how to handle defeat. They take a stab at something and when they don't succeed on the first or second attempt, they let it get to them. This is a self-defeating cycle, because, as counterintuitive as it sounds, failure leads to success. Think about it in athletic terms: the difference between an Olympic-level athlete and an everyday schmuck is that the Olympic athlete isn't afraid to try again, as many times as it takes, to get the moves right and win the game. Their success did not come instantly and without consistent hard work. There is a favorite quote of mine from Michael Jordan. You've probably heard it before, but it bears repeating: "I have missed more than 9,000 shots in my career. I have lost almost 300 games. On 26 occasions I have been entrusted to take the game winning shot, and I missed. I have failed over and over and over again in my life. And that is why I succeed."[35]

I know, that's easier said than done. Grit is an acquired skill. The more you practice coping with defeat in a constructive way, the easier future failures will be to handle and overcome. *Frustration tolerance* is your secret weapon. You cannot learn grit overnight, but with a few tweaks to your perspective and strategy, defeat will no longer affect you as strongly as it used to.

REFRAMING YOUR IDEA OF DEFEAT

Defeat is not the end. Remember when you were a kid, and things that seem insignificant now felt like the most important things in the world? You might not even remember that time you flunked a quiz or got turned down by that one girl you asked out. Ten years down the line, you'll be looking at your early job stumbles the same way.

Knock on wood, you've got a hundred years to build something and find success, and your career is one part of that. You have a long time as a young person to screw up, learn from it, and grow. All the things you learn along the way will make you a better person in the future. You'll learn about who you are through these experiences. Nobody's path to success is a straight shot out of the gate, so don't hold yourself to an impossible standard. Failure is not universe-ending, even when it feels like it is.

Point of fact, you can also start collecting your "best" examples of failure. These can be useful in reframing your mindset and can be excellent fodder for job interviews. Remember those interview questions we discussed in Chapter 5? An interviewer may ask for an example of failure and what you learned from it. Every time this happens to you, write it down. Reframe it as, "Last time I did this I learned XYZ from it, and now I know a better way. Next time, I will do better."

WHAT'S THE WORST THAT COULD HAPPEN?

This is one of my favorite questions to ask—both of myself and of others. We humans are great at catastrophizing. It's easy to get spun out over the possibility of a negative outcome, and before we know it, we've gone directly from A to Z without taking the time to think rationally. This is a trap. Instead, you should take this opportunity to make it a learning moment.

Getting stuck in the trap of catastrophizing can be a self-fulfilling prophecy. It itself becomes catastrophic. If you are spinning out, and only thinking about the worst, you can start making some terrible life decisions. I've seen people stuck in this trap who ended up quitting their jobs, breaking up with significant others, or any number of other things while trying to stay "in control" or "ahead of the problem." They made life-altering decisions assuming the worst—that they would get fired, or lose everything, or whatever, but without waiting to find out all the information.

This is bad. But just as bad is the problem of decision-paralysis. You are so worried about the various outcomes, you become a deer in the headlights. Instead of rushing into the wrong decision (still bad), you make no decision at all (also bad). You let things fall where they may with no interaction or attempt to address the problem on your end. Both these scenarios can be catastrophic—thus fulfilling your prophecy. So what should you do instead? First, take a breath. Then, ask yourself a simple question.

Whenever you face a setback, or even the possibility of a setback, practice asking yourself: *What's the worst that could happen?* If you don't get the job, if you don't get the promotion, what's the worst that could happen? Let's say you lose your house and end up on the streets? Okay, what's the second-worst thing that could happen?

Maybe you don't end up on the streets, but you have to move back in with your parents. What's the third-worst thing that could happen? Maybe you don't move back in with your parents, but you have to settle for a lower-paying job to make ends meet while you figure out a new plan.

Do you see where I'm going with this? The trick is to work backward. Odds are, the most likely outcome isn't the worst outcome, which means that failure usually isn't the end of the world. This is a good exercise to reel yourself back in, step away from the edge, and ground yourself. You can handle a lot more than you think ... including defeat. These various scenarios are unlikely to happen. But even if one does, by addressing it mentally, you are also preparing your mind for how you will handle it. And sometimes these "worst scenarios" are the ones that turn out to be your greatest opportunities. Remind yourself that you have desired skills and you will figure out a new path. Failure is temporary.

WHAT TO DO WHEN YOU GET REJECTED (AND YOU WILL)

Don't play the blame game. It's tempting to put the responsibility for rejection on someone else. "It's the interviewer's fault because he didn't ask the right questions." "It's the company's fault because their requirements didn't line up with my skills." "The recruiter didn't like the way I looked, my practice interviews didn't prepare me well enough, they skipped over the most important parts of my résumé ..."

I could go on and on, and so could you, but guess what: *excuses don't change the fact that you didn't get the job.* It's true that there are aspects of the hiring process that you can't control but projecting your failure onto those things won't help you, and if the problem *is* with you, then you're going to get the same result time after time.

You can either get frustrated, or you can use this as an opportunity to advance yourself. It's up to you.

Look to your mentors. This is why it's important to have people in your corner whose opinions you value. Again, we will cover this topic in more detail in Chapter 7. Ask them for their honest opinion about your shortcomings and their suggestions for improvement. This can be especially helpful if you feel stuck but aren't sure what you're doing wrong. They've had to learn these lessons, too, so it's worth asking what worked and what didn't work for them during their own journeys.

Allow yourself to be bummed out—just not for long. Rejection can be devastating, especially when it means saying goodbye to a job you had your sights on for a long time. I don't think anyone should be expected to be a soulless machine, which is why I want you to take the time to be bummed out ... to an extent. Do what you need to do to take care of yourself. It's okay to spend a day or two mourning what could have been, but if you wallow in self-pity for too long, you risk stalling out.

You might feel like there's no point anymore, and that you'll never find another opportunity like the one you lost, but you're wrong. The sooner you get back to your search, the sooner you'll stumble on that next big thing, so don't waste too much time feeling sorry for yourself. Pick yourself up, dust yourself off, and dive back in. Remember: it's only over when you decide it is.

Resolve to do better. Another great way to handle failure is to reclaim it. Actively decide to take this as a learning experience and add it to your arsenal. Embrace your mistakes instead of sweeping them under the rug. Most importantly, use them as motivation to improve yourself. Return to your list of role models and career goals for added inspiration and reaffirm your dedication. Remember, if success were easy, then everyone would be successful.

Adjust your approach. Examining failure is important because it allows us to correct our course. It's okay to fail over and over, but not if you're failing the same way every time. If something isn't working, don't waste time waiting for things to suddenly fall into place. Instead, change up the way you're handling the situation. You will find that you continually need to evolve with the times.

Look for patterns. Where are you getting stuck? Are you making it into the latter stages of the hiring or promotion process, only to drop out of the running? Maybe your skills aren't competitive enough yet, or you're not selling yourself well enough face-to-face. Are you having trouble even getting that first interview? It could be that your cover letter is formulaic and isn't getting the attention of the hiring manager. By figuring out where in the process you're getting tripped up, you have a clearer starting point for improvements.

Make an action plan. Once you've got a good idea of what isn't working, make a list of action items for improvement. It can be overwhelming to want to change your whole approach at once, so break it down into steps that are easy to take. These could be as simple as having someone look over your résumé and cover letter, practicing your self-presentation, or adjusting which skills and experience to emphasize. You won't be able to overhaul your abilities overnight, so focus on the things you can change right now.

FINDING THE OPPORTUNITY IN FAILURE

Often, the biggest chances for growth and self-improvement take the form of defeat. Every attempt, whether or not it's successful, is a form of practice, and every failure puts you one step closer to your goal.

When you step back and examine the path that led you to a setback, you have the opportunity to figure out what works and what doesn't, then course correct.

What lessons can I learn from this? This is something I want you to get in the habit of asking yourself. Sometimes, the answer is obvious. If you know you didn't make the cut because you bombed the interview, then this is your chance to reassess how you present yourself and your abilities. Was a client or customer unhappy with something specific you did? Own that mistake and take that lesson to heart. There is a book I really love—*Extreme Ownership* by Jocko Willink and Leif Babin, both of whom served as US Navy SEALs. Taking ownership of both failures and successes is one of the secrets to success in the SEALs and, really, in life. As they say in their book, "Implementing Extreme Ownership requires checking your ego and operating with a high degree of humility. Admitting mistakes, taking ownership, and developing a plan to overcome challenges are integral to any successful team."[36]

Sometimes, though, the path for growth isn't clear, so here are two questions to get you thinking.

- **What are my weaknesses? What are my strengths?** Think back to how you found your niche and repeat the process. What feedback, positive or negative, have you received in school or previous jobs? Take this opportunity to rank your top five overall strengths and weaknesses and consider having your mentor do the same. Own it. Are they the same? Find out why or why not. Then pick one weakness and start addressing it: Starting reading about the issue, finding new ways to approach the problem, or even reach out for help from a therapist if necessary. When ready, start working on the next, and so on.
- **Do my strengths and weaknesses align with my approach?** A single setback shouldn't be enough to make you change course, but sometimes it's worth reconsidering your strategy.

Concrete issues, like gaps in your experience and missing expertise, could be preventing you from getting that job right now, but that doesn't mean you can't get it eventually. You may just need to find a way to fill in those weak points before you apply again for another similar position. There may also be a more fundamental mismatch. Are you sure you're really passionate about what you're aiming for, or are you just doing what you feel like you "should" be doing? Are you an introvert when your dream role requires you to be a people person? Take a step back and think about your situation from all angles, seeking outside opinions where you can. You may need to rethink your goals or the path you're taking to reach them.

- **Do I let this make me stronger or weaker?** What you practice is what you become, and that's especially true when things don't go your way. If you constantly react to setbacks with frustration, rage, and depression, that eventually becomes your go-to response. The same goes for reacting to setbacks with grace, optimism, and curiosity. These skills are best learned early on in your career, and they apply to every other speed bump that life throws at you, both inside and outside of the workplace.

Failure sucks, but it's also universal. Whether that failure is rejection from a job you wanted, being passed over for a promotion, or having to go back to the drawing board in your career—sometimes more than once, like I did, your responsibility to yourself is not to let it destroy you. The past is immutable, but the future is in your hands, so why not use your time to give yourself the best shot at success that you can?

There is one opportunity that always exists in any negative experience, and that is the opportunity to get back up. Even if you get nothing else out of a rejection, you always get the choice whether to build grit or destroy it. That choice is yours.

#PACE PROCESS STEPS

- **Apply. Apply. Apply.** Apply to jobs, apply your skills in new ways, apply yourself to everything you do.
- **Reframe your negative self-talk.** Change your doubts and assumptions into something more realistic and constructive, instead of taking them at face value.
- **Take time to appreciate your achievements.** Remind yourself of your victories as often as you can, especially when your self-confidence is at a low point.
- **Take control of what you can change and accept the things you can't.** Don't always focus on the long-term; focus on actions you can take right now to improve your odds of success.
- **Make a game plan.** You can't predict the future, but you *can* prepare for it. Maintain a strong support system, brush up on your skills, build your network, and keep your eyes open for new opportunities—even if you aren't actively searching.
- **Change your perspective.** Ask yourself what the worst possible outcome of failure could be, and then work backward. Whatever your "end of the world" scenario is, it likely won't be what ends up happening.
- **Own your mistakes and failures.** Give yourself a chance to feel crappy, and then move on, without wasting time blaming your failure on others. You can't change the past, but you can change the future, so focus on what you *can* do moving forward to improve your odds in the next round.

- **Discuss the issue with your mentors.** Don't be ashamed to reach out to people you trust and respect. Be honest. Ask them for genuine feedback about your progress, abilities, and weaknesses. Pick their brains about their own experiences and failures, and what they did to overcome them.
- **Look for the lessons in failure.** This is your chance to take inventory. What are your strengths and are you leveraging them the best way you can? What are your weaknesses and are they crippling you?
- **Decide how you handle defeat.** Every time something doesn't go your way, you can choose to let it make you stronger or weaker. Get back up, address the issue, and use failure as motivation to do better in the future.

SECTION 3
COMMIT

#PACE: PREPARE + APPLY + **COMMIT** + EXPLORE

CONGRATULATIONS! YOU'VE DONE IT. You've done the work and put in the time, you've leveraged your connections, perfected your application package, and you killed it at your interview (maybe even more than one). The call comes in: you've got the job! The offer is official, and you're being invited to start immediately. All you have to do now is say yes, and then you're in the clear, right?

No—or rather, not quite. Not if you're being thoughtful about how you address your career. Of course, if you want to say yes right off the bat, hang up, and not think about it anymore, there's nothing stopping you. I can't say I blame you either. Job hunting is exhausting, time-consuming, and emotionally draining, and the first instinct on getting an offer is to wash your hands of the whole process. The problem is that you can't lose your sense of direction or focus when it comes to your career, and this becomes *even more important* once the job offers start coming in. That's why we're going to discuss what to do once you've gotten that first yes, and how to best think about your job once you've made it past the threshold.

It's easy to dismiss your first "real" job as just a way to get off the ground, especially when you're in your twenties and early thirties and feel like the world is full of possibilities. It's true that as a young adult, you have ample room to make mistakes and get your hands dirty, and you should feel free to experiment, reflect, and broaden your horizons. But you have to find balance. You need to understand that this is a very important period in your career. Your first couple of jobs will not only show you what you like, what you're good at, and what you ultimately want to do in your career, but they will also set the stage for everything that comes after. It is important to not take just *any* job. You need to be mindful of those goals you worked so hard to define in Sections 1 and 2.

There's a choice to be made once you enter the workforce: will you direct your career, or will you let your career direct you? If you mindlessly move through work early on in your career—just going through the motions like you did to get that B in economics—you're wasting valuable time to kickstart an influential path, and you're setting yourself up for future struggles.

This is your opportunity to carefully consider the job you take. This section is all about *committing*. You are likely (barring disaster) going to be in this position for at least a year, and likely with this company for several years. To find success, you are going to have to commit to making the most of it and utilizing every opportunity that comes your way.

CHAPTER 7
ONCE YOU'RE IN

CREATING A MINDFUL CAREER ROADMAP

My friend, Jennifer Tice, works in talent development and mentors young adults. When I asked her about the trends she'd been seeing, she said to me, "The kids I coach cast these super wide nets. That's not how you run your career. You have to be mindful about the next choice you make, so you won't be surprised where the next choice leads." One choice leads to another, in work and in life. That's why backing up and examining your path is so essential. By creating a career roadmap and examining it with direction and intent, you can gain the clarity you need to follow through, or adjust, when it's necessary.

Choice can be hard. Myriad studies prove choice is hard, and the more choices you have, the more you experience "decision fatigue." That's why your career map is so important. It is your opportunity to sit down and make those choices from a clearheaded, rested mental space. That's not to say those choices won't change throughout time; this is just a starting point. As you progress through your career, there will be more and more choices. Having this roadmap to reference can again help keep you clearheaded. However, if you have to make a decision in the moment or in a high-stress environment, there are a few things you can do to help yourself. According to Leslie Ye's article "The Psychology of Choice: How to Make Easier Decisions," Sheena Iyengar, a professor at Columbia Business School who studies choice, has five tips that we have extrapolated to make them applicable to your situation.[37]

1. **Cut: When faced with a daunting quantity of options,** less really is more. Try to find the right balance of options— enough to where you make an informed decision, but not so many that you are overwhelmed.

2. **Make Things Concrete:** Understand the consequences of your choices (including the choice to do nothing.) Feel the consequences in vivid ways so you don't make impulse decisions.

3. **Categorize:** Put your options into categories to make comparisons easier. Don't try to compare radically different features of jobs, benefits, or other. It won't work. Look at each element individually.

4. **Condition for Complexity:** Start with the easy decisions and build up from there. Once the simple choices are out of the way, you make handling the harder ones easier.

5. **Set a Deadline:** "Parkinson's Law theorizes that work expands to fill the time available for completion. So, if you have a 5:00 p.m. deadline, you'll work until 5:00 p.m. If you have a 2:00 p.m. deadline, you'll get the same amount of work done by 2:00 p.m." Give yourself a deadline for any decision and *stick to it.*

Now, using these tips, let's get back to your roadmap. Where do you see yourself in three, five, or ten years? It's a cliché, but it's also a good question, and one you'll want to answer before you end up going down a path that doesn't work for you. Remember the reflections you did Bootstrapping 101, and then go deeper. Think about your dream job: What does it look like? Does it have a title? Will you be working remotely, in the office, or some level of both (hybrid)? How you work is an important question right now, especially as companies are offering more options for their employees. What kind of an impact are you having on the world and on other people? Are you working at a big company or a small business? Are you freelancing? Consulting? Managing? Figure out as many specifics as you can. Compensation is also a factor. For some people, the money is a top priority. For others, the salary is less important than the chance to gain experience and rise through the ranks. There's no wrong answer, but it's important to consider these things early on, so you know what to shoot for. Remember, start with the easy decisions and work up to the hard ones.

Start with big-picture concepts for the next three years. Then do five years. And then ten. Don't worry about the details yet. We will look at the small steps a little later. For right now, the big picture is what matters because it will affect whether you take this first job offer or not.

- **How do you want to work?** Here's where you get to be picky. *How* you work is just as important as what kind of work you do. It's easy to say, "In ten years I'll be the CEO of a Fortune 500 company," but you should also think about what that entails. Just because something sounds impressive on paper doesn't mean that it's a practical fit for *you*.

If you're not a people person, then managing an entire team might not be the right goal for you. If you don't like having a rigid schedule and want to make your own hours, take that into account and work toward a consultant position or entrepreneurship. Do you prefer to work from home? Find a company that will allow you to grow internally from the comfort of your own house, keeping in mind that you need to be disciplined and practice self-accountability and project management. Think about what you want from your ideal work situation early on in your career and ask yourself whether your aspirations mesh with those requirements.

- **Solve for X.** Once you have an idea of your dream job, it's time to fill in the space between where you are right now and where you want to end up. This will look different for everyone, so do some research. What kind of experience do you need in order to advance? How well does it line up with the work you're doing now? Work backward, thinking about the steps you'll need to take. For example:
  - » Dream job: Vice President of Product
    - » Step 1. Associate Product Manager
    - » Step 2. Product Manager
    - » Step 3. Senior Product Manager
    - » Step 4. Director of Product
    - » Step 5. Vice President of Product
- **Fill in the gaps.** It's time to dig deeper. For every role on your roadmap, make a checklist of requirements. What are the minimum qualifications? Do you have the right degree or will you need additional certifications? How many years of experience are required? What kinds of soft skills

are needed? While you progress in your career, return to this list and cross things off as you grow and learn. Some requirements will take longer to meet than others, but periodically returning to this list will help you stay on track and keep tabs on what you're missing in order to get from Point A to Point B. Using the above example, an Associate Product Manager job may require a Bachelor's degree in a relevant field and one to two years of related experience:

Associate Product Manager qualifications:

» Bachelor's degree in a relevant field

» 1 to 2 years of relevant experience

» Technical expertise (e.g., engineering)

Product Manager qualifications:

» Bachelor's degree in a relevant field

» 3 to 5 years of product management experience

» Strong problem solving, research, and data analysis skills

Senior Product Manager qualifications:

» MBA in a relevant field

» 5+ years of product management experience

» Proven leadership skills

» Ability to make data-driven management decisions

Director of Product qualifications:

» MBA in a relevant field

» 5+ years of product management experience

» 5+ years of leadership experience

» Outstanding team management ability

» Relevant certifications (for example, DAVSC, CPM, MSDi, and so on)

VP of Product qualifications:

>> MBA in a relevant field

>> 8+ years of relevant experience

>> Ability to lead cross-functionally with
other departments

>> Relevant certifications (for example, DAVSC, CPM,
MSDi, and so on)

>> Demonstrated experience developing and shipping
successful products

By clearly identifying the most crucial components of each position, you can see exactly which areas you need to focus on and which steps you need to take in order to advance.

Once you've made your map, take a step back and look at where you are right now. Consider very carefully what experience you're getting in your current job or would be getting if you accepted the open job offer. Think back to your interview, and what your day-to-day responsibilities will look like if you accept the role. If this job isn't a step on your roadmap, then will you be doing work that will help you get on track? How much of what you're doing or what you will be doing can be applied to your dream job? If the answers to these questions are "not much" or "none," that's a sign that you need to think about declining the offer, or, if you're already working, that you need to start looking for a better opportunity. Keep in mind that experience trumps titles. A low-level but relevant job is more useful to you in the long run than a high-level job that's ultimately irrelevant—that is why you will often see people take a step out of their role and start at a lower title and pay to advance further in another career path.

Remember, this isn't just for when you're starting out. You should repeat this process with every new job offer, opportunity, or promotion that comes your way. Sometimes, turning that offer down is better for your long-term goals. Always be asking yourself what saying yes will mean, what doors it will open, and which paths it will cut off. You may not always know, and that's fine, but always try to look at the big picture. The course of your career is in your hands, so don't let yourself be pushed onto a road that you don't want to be on.

A "YES" IS ONLY HALF THE BATTLE

It's tempting to just want to shout out a big happy "YES!" when you get the job you want. But don't. *Seriously.* If you've already thought long and hard about what this role will mean for your career, giving an immediate answer is all right, but it is highly recommended to take some time to mull it over. This is doubly important when you have—or are expecting—multiple job offers. Instead of responding in the heat of the moment, reiterate your enthusiasm about the job and ask when the hiring manager needs a response. Be clear that you're very interested, but tell them that you would like some time, even just a few days, to weigh your options. If you're polite and professional, there's nothing wrong with taking some extra time to think things over. If nothing else, it shows that you're mature, measured, and thoughtful.

Notify your network—but not right away. This sounds counterintuitive, but you don't want to update your social media and put out an announcement the second you receive a job offer. What if you don't end up taking it? That doesn't look good for your personal brand. If you've done your due diligence and kept your eyes peeled for bad signs, it's less likely, but there's always a chance that things won't work out. Quick job changes can raise eyebrows when you broadcast them, so don't jump the gun until you're sure you'll be accepting the job. This holds true even once you accepted the job. Give yourself some time to make sure it's the right fit before you announce anything.

Weigh your options. If you've received multiple offers, carefully consider your options. There is the potential that you can negotiate the terms at your first choice job by leveraging an offer from another company. This can be a risky move, so if you try it, make sure you do so very respectfully. Go back to the hiring manager and say you'd really like to take the offer, but you were wondering if there was any flexibility in the offer because you did receive a very attractive offer from another company. It may be that they will work with you.

As a point of note: your next step will be to read your contract carefully BEFORE you notify other companies that you have accepted a position. Don't say anything until that contract is signed. We are going to go into that in the next section, but I want to make it clear that the following points in this section actually should come after the contract. But they are related here, so I've included them even though it's a bit out of order.

Let other prospective employers know. Once you've made a final decision and signed a contract, don't leave the other companies hanging. Giving other hiring managers a heads up isn't just professional—it's the right thing to do. Ghosting them could really come back to hurt you. Do this once, and that hiring manager will remember. Even if they move to a new company. And the company itself may flag your name and blackball you in the future.[38] Don't compromise your professional brand like that. Compose a polite email to everyone who's sent you an offer, as well as those you're still waiting to hear back from, explaining that you've accepted another role. It could look like this:

> *I'm writing to thank you sincerely for considering me for the role of [POSITION]. It was an absolute pleasure speaking with you to discuss your organization and this*

generous opportunity. I have ultimately decided to withdraw my application, since I have accepted another position that I believe is a better fit for my skills and experience. Thank you again for your consideration and taking the time to speak with me. I hope to work with you at some point in the future, and wish you and your company all the best.

Thank the person who hired you. Take a few minutes to send a brief email to whomever offered you the position, as well as to your new manager, if appropriate. It can be short and sweet, just like the emails you send to new people in your network: a few lines thanking them for the opportunity and reiterating your excitement about the company, the role, and the work you'll be doing. It's an easy thing to do, but it means a lot, and it reinforces the hiring manager's decision to take a chance on you. Here's a sample thank you:

I wanted to thank you for your incredibly generous offer of the [POSITION] position. I'm thrilled to be able to join your organization and work with a team as dynamic, dedicated, and enthusiastic as the team at [COMPANY NAME]. I appreciate all the time you spent discussing the job with me, and I'm excited to dive into the role. Thank you again for this incredible opportunity, and I look forward to speaking more with you in the coming weeks!

READ YOUR CONTRACT!!!

The next step (prior to turning down other offers) is to ask to see your employment contract. This is an essential, and extremely neglected, part of the process. You need to read your contract word for word. I really can't stress this enough. This is your final opportunity to vet the company you will be working for, as well as to understand their policies, benefits, and the expectations for your new role. It may be that the role they advertised doesn't match up with that which is described in your contract. That is a huge red flag. And you need to be careful to make sure you are fully aware of what you are signing up for.

This is also an opportunity to negotiate. As a standard practice, you should always negotiate. Don't be afraid to ask for what you deserve. They may come back and say it's a "take it or leave it" deal, but the more they need you the more they will be willing to meet you halfway. As Sophie Theen, HR expert, told me, "It depends on how critical that role is and if it's a role that's easily replaceable with lots of people in the pipeline. If so, then I would 100 percent say, the employer would just say no, it's a take it or leave it. But on the other hand, employees should also really, really, really always try to negotiate regardless."[39] Perhaps you fill a gap for them. Or you have a unique skill. Or fill some other need. If that's the case, you have negotiating power. Use it!

The other big factor is you need to truly understand your rights. Your contract will delineate your benefits, any requirements for giving notice, the company's ability to terminate your employment and for what reasons, and many other pieces of essential information. If you need to, run it by someone you trust. See if the terms are reasonable. Make sure you aren't being taken advantage of by the company. It happens all too often, and the only way these companies will learn is if employees like you pay attention and speak up for what you want and deserve.

Remember, you need to take ownership of your career. Part of that means doing the necessary, but admittedly sometimes boring, job of carefully reading that contract. This would also be a good time to have an outsider's perspective. Ask trusted parents or teachers, or other mentors to review it and see if it raises any red flags for them. They have a wealth of experience and may see something you miss.

THE 90-DAY PLAN

Now that you've thoroughly assessed your goals, aspirations, and plans for success, and you've decided that this job will help you get closer to your dream role, and you've told the hiring manager that you're in and you've *read* and signed your contract. Congratulations! You're well on your way now, and you've earned the right to celebrate your success. Allow yourself to be happy, and yes, relieved.

A lot of people underestimate the importance of the first few weeks and months at a new job. It's an easy trap to fall into; you're still learning the ropes of the work, getting to know your boss and coworkers, and you probably haven't been given big responsibilities yet. The "real" work usually doesn't start the minute you walk through the door on your first day, which is why so many new hires write this period off altogether. That's the wrong move. This first learning period when you start in a new role is *exactly* when you need to roll up your sleeves and start learning everything you can. I'm not saying you need to be a genius, or magically know all there is to know right off the bat, but the learning period is a golden opportunity to show your team who you are and wasting it is doing yourself a major disservice. Here are a few action items to guide you as you start out.

UNDERSTANDING THE 90-DAY PLAN

This is the ideal way to set yourself up for success in your new job. Your employer will likely have a 90-Day Plan for you. It will cover your onboarding, acclimating you to your team, and making sure you understand what you will be expected to learn and any expected deliverables. They want you to be successful because that brings success to the team and the company.

A company's 90-Day Plan will likely include the following: setting you up in their payroll system, setting you up with their network and email systems, introducing you to your team, assigning your first tasks, attending any training programs they offer, and they will also likely schedule a check-in meeting to ensure you've met all of those milestones. This sounds tedious, I know. But it really is an opportunity for you, and you should fully participate and commit to the process.

However, their plan may look a little different from the one you create for yourself, but you will have several of the same goals. Both plans are to help you find success. That said, your goals will likely include things like making connections with colleagues, finding an internal mentor,learning their products and systems (especially in remote work), finding your way around the facility (for in-person work), etc.

YOUR 90-DAY PLAN: FIRST 30 DAYS

- **Familiarize yourself with your environment.** I'm not just talking about knowing where your office is. By getting to know the ins and outs of where you'll be spending the majority of your working hours, you're saving yourself hassle and wasted time later on. Where's the parking garage? Do you have to sign in? Is there a cafeteria, or will you need to get outside food? What important facilities should you be aware of? Make sure you understand what software, websites, and programs you'll be using, and remember to ask questions early on. It's better to get clarification as a new employee than later, when you'll be expected to already know that information.

- **Get to know your coworkers.** I cannot stress this enough. At a minimum, do your best to cultivate a relationship with the people with whom you'll be working the most closely. I'm not saying you need to be best friends with everyone in the office, but if you make an effort to form connections, and build a network, those around you will notice. The way you interact with those around you contributes to your reputation in the workplace and can open up possibilities including promotions or networking opportunities. Set a goal of learning the names of one or two coworkers a day, and don't be afraid to socialize. These acquaintances will be more likely to be available when you need help in the future.

- **Complete any training programs you are required to complete, or that are offered as optional.** This is an opportunity to take the initiative to learn more than they require. It's also an opportunity for you to show your initiative. However, I caution you to not go overboard on this. Do not do optional training to the exclusion of the job you were hired to do. This will likely be a continuous endeavor, but you can get started in the first thirty days.

YOUR 90-DAY PLAN: 30 – 60 DAYS

- **Establish your goals and prioritize them.** Your supervisor will probably throw a lot of information your way when you start out, and it's easy to get overwhelmed. Don't be afraid to have them reiterate key components of your work. A good manager will be willing to answer clarifying questions, so don't be shy if you don't understand something. Your mission here isn't to know everything perfectly and at the drop of a hat, but to distill the most important pieces of your day-to-day work into several key responsibilities. Prioritizing will help you get into a working rhythm and keep you from being blindsided later. Take notes, and consider making a list at the end of each day during your training: what are the three most important tasks? What points did your manager make more than once?

- **Figure out where your weak points are.** This will take some time and introspection, but even in the beginning, you may start to get a sense of what parts of the job will be the most challenging for you. If a gap in your skills or expertise jumps out at you, *don't panic.* Instead, think about what actions you can take to enhance your command of your responsibilities. If you're not familiar with spreadsheets or HTML coding, set some time aside to practice, watch tutorials, or ask for guidance. If your knowledge of an aspect of the industry is questionable, make a point to do some research. You don't have to be perfect from the start, but the sooner you gain control of your weak areas, the sooner you'll be able to compensate … and you won't have to wait for a negative performance review to find out where those gaps are.

This is also how you will start expanding the scope of your role. Make sure you are volunteering for any opportunities that are offered. Take the jobs no one else wants. Those jobs are often good learning opportunities, and if you can find a way to make them easier, or faster, make sure to tell your leader. When Brad Johnson was at Wayfair, he used to do the most amazing thing. As he told me, "After ninety days, I always have new employees come back to me and explain how they could eliminate any part of their job or do it better. Automate it. Systemize it. Find ways to creatively work themselves out of it. Honestly, it became a little bit of a fun game. I always promised them that if they eliminate their own job, I'd promote them."[40]

Now that is one heck of a promise! While you likely won't be able to eliminate your job fully, but if you figure out ways to do it better and can articulate that to your manager, they will take notice, I assure you.

- **Keep a lookout for red flags.** You aren't married to your new job, and if something is rubbing you the wrong way, don't ignore it. Your instincts will often be the most important compass you have. I'm not saying that you should back out the minute things get tough, but it's not unheard of for companies to misrepresent themselves and the responsibilities of a role. If there's a glaring management problem or a dysfunctional team, you may not know until you've started. The best option is always to look for a solution to the problem, but if that's not possible (and it may not be, if you're new), don't ever feel like you should ignore your gut.

This can be especially important in cases where a company is "filling a gap." Unfortunately, as Sophie Theen points out, many companies see this as the easiest way to address DE&I issues.[41] They notice a lack of diversity and they think they can just hire a couple people to fill those gaps. This thinking is shallow, and employees in this situation will often lack the support they need within the company to succeed. Be aware of this and don't be afraid to try to work the problem from the inside if possible. Ask for the necessary support systems, ask for more formal DE&I policies, and start your own groups within the company. This also shows your initiative and commitment to finding success within the company, and it will benefit those who follow.

90-DAY PLAN: 60 - 90 DAYS

- **Find an internal mentor.** Within the first ninety days of your new job, you should also be looking for a mentor, or even two. What I recommend is finding one inside your company and one outside. Both can be difficult to find but finding the right mentor inside the company is a bit more difficult, so we will start there.

  First, you need to think about what you want in a mentor. What is your motivation? Do you want to find a sense of community within the workplace? Or do you want a mentor who can help you get to your dream job? Both are valid, but are very different. If you are searching for a sense of community, you are looking for peers and superiors with whom you share common identities. But you may not be able to find someone just like you in the company. There may not be anyone else on your team that is the same gender, religion, race, or share any other identity you may have. *And that's okay.*

  Don't be afraid to seek out a mentor completely different from you in age, background, or ethnicity, or someone who is on a completely different career path. The goal in finding an internal mentor is someone who can help you navigate your way through the company. Someone who can support you, give unbiased feedback, and provide *a different perspective.* In the current political landscape, people have become afraid of other perspectives. They have an all or nothing mentality: anyone who believes differently is the enemy. You have to rid yourself of that idea and instead seek to understand even when you don't agree. Remember, a mentorship is not about just taking. You need to provide value to your mentor as well. And that can come in the form of your own unique perspective or skills you have that they lack. All relationships are give-and-take, and a mentorship is no different.

- **Find an external mentor.** The same ideas about internal mentors apply to external mentors. These are people that might be in the same industry but not at your company. Or just someone you respect that has a lot of life experience. They can help you with an outsider's perspective of issues that arise at work. Just make sure not to share confidential information. An outside mentor can be a bit easier to find, but my advice is to find someone that you can work with long-term, over the span of many years, and different companies and jobs.

  » A final note on mentors: when the time comes, step up to be a mentor for others.

- **Master Office Politics.** As a new employee, you are jumping into an existing world of office politics. There are relationships, backstories, grudges and more that you will have no awareness of, but which your colleagues will be very familiar with. This can be tricky. Office politics can be a treacherous aspect of work (especially for introverts!). My advice is to be aware of these influences and develop your own strategy for dealing with them professionally. Try to keep yourself apart from them as much as possible. Don't engage in the negative but rather make friends, keep a record of your work, and don't retaliate—just make sure they can't do it again.[42]

- **Volunteer for new initiatives.** Above, we discussed volunteering for tasks no one else wanted. Now that you are getting more firmly established in your role, you should start volunteering for new initiatives and projects. This is another opportunity to stand out, but these are the projects that often get picked up for increased funding, and the creation of new teams, opening you up to promotion possibilities more quickly.

  This is also a task that many people find to be extremely difficult. Maybe you're introverted and have trouble putting yourself forward for something, even when you really want it. Or perhaps you were in the military where volunteering was trained out of you in favor of just taking orders (or because you volunteered once and that was enough!). Whatever your reasons, many people find this difficult, but it's a skill you need to master.

  Whether you are at the start of your career or more established, you should make every effort to volunteer for new projects. This shows initiative for one, but it also offers you the opportunity to get in on the ground floor of a project that could make it big. Having a willingness to step up can be a game-changer in your career. There are, however, two big caveats. First: Don't overpromise. If you are already swamped with other projects, don't take on more than you can handle. If you can't deliver, or even over deliver on the expectations, you'll do more harm than good. Second: only take on projects that make sense for your career path. If it doesn't serve your goals (go back to that 3/5/10 year plan), then what purpose does it serve other than to burn you out and make you hate your job? Working on a project that is radically different from what you typically do and does not correlate with your career map doesn't serve your goals. Sometimes it will still be necessary, and your company will ask you to step up, but try to limit that. The key is to just always be on the lookout for the right opportunities and take them on whenever possible.

- **Join professional groups.** Your company may have all kinds of social groups and communities that are available. There are often women's groups, DE&I groups, and so on. If there isn't one you want to join, start one of your own!

- **Ask for your 90-day review.** At the end of the ninety days, make sure you ask for that meeting with your manager (if it isn't already offered to you prior to that.) In fact, insist upon it. This is your opportunity to get feedback from your leaders, discuss ideas you have, and assess your successes thus far. This last point is important. Your manager is not with you every single hour of the day. If you are working remotely or in a hybrid environment, this is even more true. They may be unaware of some of your successes. This is your opportunity to remind them of those successes or make them aware of them in the first place. I suggest keeping a list as you go, a sort of master résumé that you add everything to regardless of how small—accomplishments, extra 'added-value' projects you worked on, etc. That way you don't forget the pertinent details either. Trust me, it happens. But when you speak with your manager, don't list them all; instead select a few to highlight the *impact* (saved money, time, resources, etc.) that your work meant for the business or project. *Note: this master résumé can also be used for future job applications as well.*[43]

#PACE PROCESS STEPS

- **Take a step back.** Don't cast too wide of a net. Remember, you need to be focusing on the job you want to have years down the line, not just your next job. A title is useless unless it brings you closer to where you want to be, so be mindful about what kinds of skills you're gathering in any given role. Think about the job you want later on, not just the job you want right now.

- **Create a career roadmap.** Determine where you want your career to be in three to five years. Consider how you do your best work, what kind of environment you want in your dream job, and what impact you want to make on others. Once you've found your dream job, work backward to reverse engineer a career path. This will help you better visualize the steps you need to take in order to reach your dream job.

- **Consider what you need.** Research the steps between where you are and where you want to be. Think about what abilities and experience you'll gather in the job you're considering and ask yourself whether they'll take you up the next step of your career ladder. What are the crucial components of the job you want, and how well do they mesh with what you're doing now? If they don't, then you may need to recalibrate.

- **Mind Your Skill Gap:** If you determine that there is a gap in your skills or that you're lacking the required knowledge to make that next step, start the necessary training to fill those gaps—this might take the form of an online class, working with a mentor, getting a certification, or even just buying the right book! If you don't know where to start, talk with your mentors and ask them for the top three things they would recommend you work on given your goals and roadmap.

- **Follow proper etiquette for accepting a job offer.** Give yourself some time before saying yes to consider the pros and cons of the offer, as well as how well the job fits into your life plan. Once you've decided to go for it, thank whoever hired you in an email and reiterate your excitement about the new role. Keep your network in the loop but wait to make a big announcement until you've had some time on the job to make sure it's a good fit.

- **Create your 90-Day Plan.** Learn, learn, learn. Start your job with curiosity and take the opportunity to get familiar with your coworkers, manager, everyday responsibilities, and tools. Find your mentors. Figure out what your top priorities should be, both in your day-to-day and in your long-term activities. If you notice obvious weak points, make a note of them, so you know where to focus your attention. Watch for red flags and remember that you don't have to stay in an environment that truly isn't working for you or your goals.

- **Volunteer for new projects.** Raise that hand, just always remember your two caveats: Don't overpromise and only take on projects that make sense for your career path.

- **Request your 90-Day review.** This is a golden opportunity. Some companies require this, but if they don't you need to demand that one occur. Many people find these reviews to be scary and avoid them at all costs. Don't be that person. The benefits will far outweigh the risks, I assure you.

CHAPTER 8

LEARNING AND LEVERAGING YOUR STRENGTHS

WE'VE ALREADY DISCUSSED LEARNING AND LEVERAGING your strengths on a surface level in previous sections. You should have a pretty solid understanding of the basics by this point. But this is essential for your long-term success, so we are going to go into even greater detail.

The most important aspect to finding success in your career is keeping the momentum going. Doing so requires that mindset of learning we've discussed so much. As one of my favorite actors, Morgan Freeman, said, "I'm always trying new things and learning new things. If there isn't anything more you can learn—go off and die." Harsh, but true. If you've given up, well, honestly, you wouldn't be reading this book. But there will come a time in your career when you are exhausted and all you want to do is give up. You'll be burned out and just getting by. It will happen, but my hope is by preparing for it, you will keep those thoughts to as short of a period of time as is possible.

Learning is a key element to this. You need to have an attitude of "Always be learning." We talked a bit before about reading and cultivating new hobbies. This is also a technique you can employ in your job. In whatever role you have, you should always be learning something new. Let's discuss a few that may make an impact on your daily life.

- **Colleagues.** Your relationships with your colleagues are important and should be mutually beneficial. Once you rise to a leadership role, this is even more important. By learning about your teammates, and especially your subordinates, you will learn everyone's strengths and weaknesses. Mastering your team's abilities will make your team stronger. You will know where to place people, how to get them to work together, and how to guide them to success. But this takes time. You need to start *now*, before you ever take that leadership role. Pay attention. Help others. *Always be learning.*

- **Dress for success.** There is a common saying, "Dress for the job you want, not the job you have." Most people take this literally, but it has other implications as well. Your "dress" is more than just clothes, it is your skill set, your mindset, and your personal brand. If you know you want a specific job, start learning what it requires now. Pay attention to what your mentors do and copy it. Improve on it if you can. Take extra classes on related topics and fields. Attend conferences and any educational opportunities you find. Get all applicable certifications as early as possible. But also make sure people know about all those successes. If they don't know, they can't use that information to help you.

I know one example that always makes me laugh. In his first job out of college, a young man took a job that legally required a certification. He had one year to complete it. Apart from the notice that he would be required to complete the class and pass the test, no one mentioned it again. About six months into working for the company, his boss came to him and said, "The deadline for this is coming up. We really need to get you certified and we want to allow some extra time because most people have to take the test several times before they pass." The young man was confused. He explained to his boss, "I took that test two months ago. I'm already fully certified." His boss was dumbstruck. He'd passed on the first try (even his boss hadn't managed that), but it was even more surprising that the young man hadn't said anything after passing. The young man just thought it was something to check off a list and hadn't considered other implications, which included a company-sponsored team lunch whenever a member passed the test. Furthermore, becoming certified opened new opportunities for the young man... but only if his boss knew about it and had been able to tell him about them. His initiative was impressive, but he lost out on some opportunities and some good will by keeping it to himself. Big mistake. Lesson: Dress for success.

- **Stay current on market and industry trends.** A lot of employees show up to work and do what they are told to do. They don't track market trends or know where their industry is headed. But if you stay aware, you can anticipate obstacles and industry disruption to innovate new paths forward allowing opportunities for you to shine. Good leaders pay attention to those who anticipate and solve problems before they exist. (And bad leaders will ignore the warning signs. If this is the case, it's time for you to look for another job immediately!)

- **Learning Agility.** This is something hiring managers look for in the hiring process, but just because you got the job, that doesn't mean this goes away. You will constantly need to exhibit learning agility. The ability to solve problems, find solutions on your own is an essential skill and strength. When my employees showcase this, and when they point this skill out in the course of their work and in annual reviews, I am always impressed. Especially in hybrid and remote workspaces, this is an essential skill.

Moral of the story: Stay open to every learning opportunity available. Conventional and unconventional. The more creative you get, the more you'll learn and the more you will start to enjoy the process. Finding joy in these activities will not only make it more fun, but it will also make you more effective. Marie Kondo, organizer extraordinaire, has a great book *Joy at Work* with coauthor Scott Sonenshein. While much of their book covers how to keep your workspace and digital presence tidy and organized, they have one chapter at the end that really emphasizes finding joy at work. As Scott says in the book, "Emphasize and master those activities that do bring you joy (even if you need to keep activities that don't bring joy.)"[44] A few pages later, Marie includes this gem, "Finding meaning in our daily tasks makes our job worth doing, and this leads to joy. In fact, the attitude with which we approach our work is far more important that what kind of job we have."[45] Take this attitude into every opportunity and you will be amazed what happens for you.

LEVERAGING YOUR STRENGTHS

We've talked a lot about opportunities, executive presence and personal brand, and reframing skills. Now it's time to take all those pieces and start leveraging them as an employee. Once you are firmly entrenched in your new role (past the ninety-day mark), you can start putting your talents to their full use. This will, of course, mean leveraging your skills for your specific job, and only you will know best how to do that. There are just too many industries and too many skills to cover here. Instead, we are going to focus on those skills that are universally applicable, especially those essential to hybrid and remote work.

SOFT SKILLS

Research shows that 85 percent of job success comes from having soft skills.[46] If you haven't already, you need to develop and leverage strong interpersonal relationships and communication behaviors.

Communication is essential to everything you do at your job. It will influence your relationships with colleagues, with clients, and with your boss. This can be more difficult in the remote workspace. Most communication will occur by email, Slack messaging (or similar service), texting, phone calls, and Zoom/Webex type calls, and each of these can be tricky.

According to *How to Be Great at Your Job* by Justin Kerr, (and I agree), there are six essential requirements for an awesome email: subject, deadlines, bullet points, jump to conclusions, white space, and the attachment trap.[47] Basically, be specific and be concise. Don't waste your readers' time with unnecessary information. You want to make it as easy as possible for them to just say "yes." And only include an attachment if absolutely necessary. If it can be sent in the body of the email, it should be.

Written communication offers the benefit of providing a record, which can be important. However, you also have to remember that tone can get lost in emails. Sarcasm often doesn't translate. Jokes may miss the mark. You need to be very careful how you communicate and always keep it professional.

But this also means that you need to be aware of that same potential problem from your colleagues. Don't assume their meaning. Always check to be sure. Remember, implying versus inferring are two separate things.

- Imply: to express indirectly; to involve or indicate by inference, association, or necessary consequence rather than by direct statement[48]
- Infer: to derive as a conclusion from facts or premises; guess, surmise[49]

To imply means it is coming from the speaker. They are intentionally expressing something without saying it outright. But what if they are not implying something, but you think they are? That means you are inferring information. You are guessing that there is intention behind a statement when there may not be. It's important to give others the benefit of the doubt, just as they should for you. If you are unsure, just ask for clarification. Most problems within relationships of any kind can be solved with open and honest communication. Your colleagues will respect you more for it, and they will trust you more as well.

One final note: for god's sake, don't include personal information! I can't stress this information. Your work email is NOT PRIVATE. Your company can access your work emails. There are even entire companies whose job it is to audit another company's internal communication to check for fraud, inappropriate relationships, conflicts of interest, and any other type of illegal or unethical behavior. JUST DON'T DO IT.

DEVELOPING EQ AND LEADERSHIP

What is EQ? It stands for Emotional Quotient, or more commonly, Emotional Intelligence. "This is the ability to recognize your own emotions and other people's emotions—and then use that information to guide your thinking and doing."[50] According to Daniel Goleman, your EQ is measured by five key components: self-awareness, self-regulation, social skill, empathy, and motivation.[51] We've talked a bit about some of these topics already. There are other books on this subject that go into far more detail. What I'm going to stress here is how important it is to develop this skill. EQ is just as important, if not more important, than IQ for leaders.[52]

If you hope to earn promotions and build your career, your EQ is definitely a strength you need to cultivate and leverage. You have a unique perspective, but you should also be open to other perspectives and be willing to learn from them. There is a mindset with many young people today that is very much binary—right or wrong, good or bad, etc. without allowing for shades of gray. As you get older, this becomes clearer, and you will start to recognize how divisive it is and how it holds you back from experiences. If you can empathize with others, especially those with different opinions and perspectives, you will be a stronger leader. Have the strength of character to just agree to disagree, and don't be overly sensitive and take offense at every little violation to your perfect worldview. At least, not if you want to rise to the heights in your career that you desire.

Let's go back to those five traits, directly from Goleman's original article:

1. "Self-Awareness – the ability to recognize and understand your moods, emotions, and drives, as well as their effect on others.

2. Self-regulation – the ability to control or redirect disruptive impulses and moods. The propensity to suspend judgment—to think before acting.

3. Motivation – a passion to work for reasons that go beyond money or status. A propensity to pursue goals with energy and persistence.

4. Empathy – the ability to understand the emotional makeup of other people. Skill in treating people according to their emotional reactions.

5. Social Skill – proficiency in managing relationships and building networks. An ability to find common ground and build rapport."[53]

You can read about all kinds of opinions on this subject in other books and I've already covered all of these tangentially, and some of them directly, in previous sections. So now I'm going to ask you to really sit down and consider these five topics, specifically as they apply to you. Take some time. Stop reading here, and just spend an hour on this task. Do whatever you do when you do your best thinking: go for a run, take a hot bath, go hit some balls on the driving range, or whatever it is that works for you. But really consider how you can work these five traits into your daily life.

STAND OUT

Earlier, we discussed raising your hand and volunteering for the jobs no one else wants, or for new initiatives. This is one component to standing out. We talked about it in Chapter 7 because it applied to your 90-Day Plan. But as you progress in your career, you will want to do more. Standing out can mean a lot of different things to different people. Some of these tips may not apply to you, depending on your company or your role. But some are also universal.

1. **Volunteer.** We've covered this, so I'm not going to review it again here. But one final thought about volunteering is it can also mean volunteering outside your company. Find a charity to work with. Putting your time and passion into a worthy cause can also help you stand out from your peers.

2. **Under promise and over deliver.** This is always good advice. Have realistic deadlines, and then provide your boss, client, or whomever with the deliverable ahead of schedule if you can. Sometimes you won't be able to. New information may come in, life may interfere, or something else may change. But make every effort to accomplish this every time.

3. **Don't be afraid to showcase your successes.** A lot of people feel this is bragging, but that's not what I'm talking about here. Bragging is different from accepting praise for your work. This is about making sure you receive credit for your contributions. You can't shy away from this. And certainly, never allow others to take credit you rightly deserve. Advocate for yourself.

4. **Share but don't overshare.** This is tricky. You don't need to be everyone's friend; instead, try to be *friendly acquaintances* with nearly everyone… but let's be honest, there is almost always that one person who irritates you. Just try to avoid them while always maintaining professional courtesy. And don't be a hater! Always try to share in another's good news and support them in the tough times—even the ones who irritate you.

   To build trust and rapport, you need to share aspects of your life with your colleagues, but don't overshare. Don't bring the negatives in life into work with you. Share happy news, don't brag, and stay humble. Inviting others to share in happy news makes them connect with you, and people remember that. It is another way to stand out.

CHECK IN—WITH YOURSELF AND OTHERS

Your goals are your livelihood and your mission. Being mission-focused will give you purpose, even in tough times. It's essential that you revisit your goals and career roadmap regularly. You have now completed your 3/5/10 year roadmap. Hopefully, you've also found a job and made it through your 90-Day Plan. So why are we going over this again? Because it's a journey. And journeys have mile-markers and pit stops. By now, I'm sure you understand why. What we will discuss here are some tips and tools to make it an efficient habit.

Make a folder on your desktop for these files. Your application package should be one piece: résumé, cover letter, and follow up letters should all be here. These can be constantly updated with new accomplishments, responsibilities, and tasks. Achievements are essential to track. You can do that in your résumé or create a new document specifically for that purpose with as much detail as possible. Information on month/year, team you were on, role you had (not just job title, but the specific role on the team), any tasks you took or spearheaded, and the results. Results should be as specific as possible. Percentages, raw numbers, etc.

The next file should include your 90-Day Plan and your career roadmap. The 90-Day Plan is specific to a new role or new company. This won't be updated, so I recommend starting a new one for every job and every promotion. Keep these and track your progress over time. You never know when this information will be useful. Your career roadmap should be continually updated as needed and revisited every six months. This gives you a nice period to reevaluate your goals and where you are in your life. If something big happens that alters this trajectory (bought a house, got married, had a child, moved to a new company, etc.), notate it and adjust accordingly.

The roadmap is also something you can revisit with your mentors or your spouse down the road. Sharing goals helps realize them. It makes them real, and when people are aware of your goals, they will often do what they can to help. Even saying them to yourself helps you put them into action on a subconscious level and raises your awareness of opportunities. If you're looking for a yellow car, you'll start seeing them everywhere, but you don't notice them until you bring them into focus and make it *matter*.

#PACE PROCESS STEPS

- **Always be learning**. Make an effort to learn about colleagues. Build relationships. Stay open to conventional and unconventional learning opportunities. Stay on top of market trends and dress for success!
- **Check in on your career map regularly.** This is important to stay on course. Just as navigators regularly check latitude and longitude, you need to do the same for your career map so you don't end up lost.
- **Develop those soft skills.** But be creative in your approach and find the methods that work for you. Give yourself, and others, the benefit of the doubt.
- **Reflect on how to build your EQ.** Leadership will be expected of you, if not today then someday. How you lead will be unique to you, but the building blocks are pretty much the same for everyone. Start cultivating this skill *now*.
- **Stand out.** Find what works for you. Just keep in mind that standing out sometimes also means blending in. Learn to know when you should do each.

CHAPTER 9
STAYING THE COURSE

THERE IS A LOT TO BE SAID FOR STAYING THE COURSE and committing to finding success in a company, whether it is a start-up or a Fortune-500 company. There are pros and cons to both scenarios, but wherever you are, you should be looking to your future within this company... for now. (We will discuss moving on to a new company in the next section.) For now, let's focus on high-level steps you can take as you climb that success ladder right now.

WHAT *IS* SUCCESS, ANYWAY?

Success: Noun—getting or achieving wealth, respect, or fame; the correct or desired result of an attempt; someone or something that is successful: a person or thing that succeeds.[54]

What do you think of when you hear the word "success"? It's subjective. Arbitrary, even. But deciding how you define success for yourself is crucial to finding it; after all, how will you know how to go after something if you don't know what that something is?

A lot of people assume that success is what the media proclaims it is: mansions, yachts, good looks, and millions in the bank.

Fame and fortune, in other words. But the thing I've noticed over the course of my time in the workforce is that success is as diverse as the person achieving it. Some people view success in the traditional sense of money. Others view success as having a positive impact on the world through their work. Some people view success as raising a family or earning a reputation that goes beyond just their company. Some see success as complete and total independence, not needing to rely on anyone for anything in their personal (and business) lives. To me, success is being a good father and running a business that makes a difference on the way people work.

Maybe one of these definitions speaks to you, or maybe your definition of success is entirely different. It doesn't matter. *You* are the only person who can decide what success looks like to you. Even if by all outside appearances you're finding success in your career, it doesn't matter if *you* don't feel like you're achieving your purpose and living at your fullest potential.

Think about what you want from life and ignore what everyone else wants. Think about what you want your legacy to be after you're done working. It may change over time, but make sure that it's always clear to you. This will be the lens through which you look at your career and gauge your progress, so don't get sucked into what anyone else says you *should* be aiming for. Their idea of success has nothing to do with yours.

The big question: does my current path match up with my goals?

In Chapter 2, I wrote about picturing your ideal job years down the line, and about how to decide if a current job offer will put you closer to that goal. It's an important step to getting on the right track, but there's always the possibility that things will change, even if you're doing everything right on paper. That advice also goes for when you're already well-entrenched in your job, and in some ways, that's when it's most important to be asking yourself those questions. Sometimes, the trappings of a career seem great when you're first getting started, and it's only after you've been in the industry for a few years that you see the dark side of the field you're in. Maybe the business world has shifted since you started out, and the landscape is different from what you envisioned for yourself while planning your career. You might end up like me, doing work that you never signed up for, or maybe your company has undergone drastic changes and has a mission that no longer matches your morals and values.

Balance is important, of course. Not getting along with a coworker or disliking a project you're currently working on isn't necessarily a good reason to pull the plug on your current job. Pay attention to your overall sense of well-being. When you take a step back, are you happy with the work you're doing, and if not, are you at least happy with the work you *could* be doing later on? There is a great quote from Mark Twain: "Find a job you enjoy doing, and you will never have to work a day in your life." This is *mostly* true. There are always going to be aspects of a job you don't like. But if you are passionate about what you do overall, your satisfaction and the level of fulfillment you feel will make it joyful. If something about your job *is* bugging you, ask yourself whether it's a problem with your current role, or an intrinsic feature of this field or company. For example:

- **Temporary problems:** I don't like my coworkers, I don't like my current assignment, I don't like my office, I don't like my commute.
- **Intrinsic problems:** Toxic corporate culture, company- or department-wide mismanagement, moral/ethical problems, lack of opportunity for advancement.

If a problem is specific to your current situation, then there may be a way of reworking your position without backing out of your entire role. Is it something that can be solved by working with human resources, negotiating a work-from-home role, or gritting your teeth and getting through your current project? On the other hand, if a problem is inherent to the company or industry as a whole, then it may be time to rethink your place of employment.

Until you reach that point, it's important to focus on success in the here and now.

CLIMBING THE CORPORATE LADDER

The word "ladder" is really a misnomer. The corporate ladder really isn't a ladder anymore. That probably existed back in the '50s, but that metaphor has been changing for some time now. The journey to your dream job—that job you defined in your career map as the ultimate goal—is just that… a journey. Sometimes it will move straight forward, but it may also require a few steps back at times. Or a pause to catch your breath and reflect. And it might even include a few lateral side steps to a parallel path. This doesn't mean you're not making the progress you need or that you're holding yourself back. It means you're doing it *right*.

Let's revisit my client Mike Glass. He has a perfect example of this from earlier in his career. He was climbing the ladder in a very linear fashion. He'd even recently been promoted to Senior Vice President. But one day he realized how unfulfilled he was professionally. Whereas some would take a passive approach, Mike did the opposite. Mike reached out to friends and colleagues to discuss the issue with them. He discovered an alternate career path and took deliberate steps to position himself effectively to achieve his new goal. He changed jobs and roles—some of his moves were lateral, some were steps down in title and compensation, but each role checked meaningful boxes that would enable him to realize his potential. These deliberate job rotations ultimately led to the role that Mike has now—Vice President, Global Talent for a Fortune 100 company and doing what he loves.

This is what I'm talking about when I say you're doing it the right way. Was this part of his career map? Probably not, at least not initially. Your map can change as your goals and interests change. Don't be afraid to make a lateral move or even a step down if you need to so you can find the level of fulfillment and joy in your work that you desire. Money isn't everything. It's a factor, sure. But you should define your goals outside of that as well. Remember, it is a journey, not a ladder. Climb the mountain, but don't expect it to be easy or that you'll make it to the top by following just one path. Find the courage to make your own path there.

THE ANNUAL REVIEW ADVANTAGE

The Golden Opportunity. Oh boy, I could tell you some stories about annual reviews from my own years as an employee, from friends, and from my time as the boss. If you aren't taking advantage of your annual review, then you are losing out on one of the greatest tools you have for finding success. If that's the case, then let's change it.

First, let's go over some general background on the annual review. They are designed to evaluate results of employees and teams, and while it may seem like they focus on the critical, really it is a company's way of identifying strengths and weaknesses on the whole, as well as on the individual level. This is often done through ratings, though many companies are moving away from these traditional systems which can be a mixed blessing. Quantifiable assessments and year-over-year data do have value if done correctly.

The most important aspect of annual reviews is that they drive internal mobility. That means jobs fill more quickly, and employees stay longer and are more successful in their roles. That means your potential for a raise, bonus, and promotion often lie in the annual review. But to take advantage of that, you will really need your manager to take the process seriously. Some managers just try to glide through the process with the least amount of work. This means they often avoid giving critical, constructive feedback, or that they focus only on the negative and don't give you credit for your successes. Don't let your boss get away with this. Insist on a detailed discussion if need be, and make sure your boss has properly assessed your strengths and contributions.

I know this can be a little scary and anxiety inducing, but it is also your opportunity to learn about yourself from another's perspective. It can also give you insight into your boss and the company you work for—for good and for bad. Let's look at the personal aspects first.

LEARN ABOUT YOURSELF

The annual review is a document produced by your direct boss (in most cases). This is the person who sees your work on a regular basis, assesses your relationships with your colleagues, and evaluates your progress. There are often some standard categories that are included: delivering results, problem solving, knowledge and skills, communication, collaboration, customer service, taking initiative, personal development, and an overall score. Various companies may use some or all of these or have additional ones of their own creation.

These categories can provide a lot of valuable insight into how others in the company perceive you and your work. Sometimes, this can feel very personal. But you have to remember it is not. They are interested in helping you achieve your best results. When employees succeed, the company succeeds. For the most part, your colleagues want you to succeed, too. Don't get me wrong, sometimes annual reviews can be unfairly negative. I have a friend who was reprimanded in her annual review for not participating in the company

Ping-Pong tournament, (and not because she objected to it, but because she was working sixty hours a week just to stay on top of her work and for no extra pay.) I admit, that is ridiculous and inappropriate. But even if you have a bad review, try to give people the benefit of the doubt. Try to view things through their eyes. This goes back to the idea of *Extreme Ownership*. If you made a mistake, or could have handled things better, *own it*. Own it and use it to do better.

Once you get your review, I often recommend you take some time to consider it. Don't react in the moment as that can be an emotional time. Take a breath, sleep on it, and really consider if their feedback is fair and accurate. Be humble. If a response is warranted, take the time to write it out and consider it. Don't react out of anger. Be thoughtful about how you address the concerns outlined in the review. And remember, one bad review does not a career make.

LEARN ABOUT YOUR COMPANY

The review is often a great opportunity to learn about your company and recognize any red flags. It can be a great way to see that your company is following through on their mission statement, are supportive of their employees, and genuinely interested in employee success. This can be true of both the company and your direct supervisor. Pay attention to how they are phrasing any feedback, and what kind of support they offer. If they don't, it's a red flag. The company culture can also shift throughout time, and annual reviews are a great way to identify their values and priorities, and any changes therein.

Company culture can change quickly within a company and the annual review can be an indicator. Remember that friend I told you about with the Ping-Pong tournament? Just a couple months prior she had been recognized for her contributions to the company, given a large performance bonus, and had increased her division's revenue by about 75 percent. But by her quarterly review, just three months later, her division was assigned to a new VP, the company moved to a new location, and it expanded. The company culture did a complete reversal. Now, that is not to say she hadn't made mistakes herself. She learned a few things in that annual review about herself—things that weren't necessarily easy to hear. But she also learned that her company no longer had her back. They were more interested in perception and optics than they were in results and supporting their leads. Those were major red flags that indicated it was time to move on. We'll talk about this more when it's time to move on in Section 4, but just remember, the review is an opportunity to understand where your company is headed.

WHAT YOU SHOULD DO

- Insist your manager take your annual review seriously and sit down with you to discuss it at length.
- Declare your aspirations. Make sure your boss knows what you want.
- Assess how you view your own work.
- Learn what you can do better.
- Ask for blunt advice.
- Review your annual review with one or both of your mentors. Get their feedback as well.

NEGOTIATING FOR WHAT YOU'RE WORTH

The end of the annual review is also your opportunity to negotiate for an appropriate raise, just like you negotiated when you were reading your contract. First off, any credible company should automatically give you a cost-of-living raise based on a variety of factors in your region. Usually, the local government will announce what that rate is based on their internal statistics and demographics. If your company doesn't offer you that much, it's another red flag. Perhaps there are mitigating factors where you could forgive it one year. But if it is consistent year over year, then you should be concerned.

You should also be negotiating a raise with every promotion and every annual review. Learning how to negotiate is an important step in your career. You and your skills are valuable. You need to be able to articulate your contributions to the company in a way that makes them recognize and reward the value you are providing. Just as you are committing to them, you want to make sure they are committed to you as an employee. As you contemplate career moves to new positions, and/or new companies, you also need to be cognizant of the compromises you will be making. Just like you negotiate for your salary, you will need to negotiate for the right job for you and your career roadmap.

CAREER COMPROMISES AND TRADE-OFFS

As I was writing this book, I spoke with several high-profile talent management executives about young adults currently entering the workforce. The underlying concern they all had in common was that young professionals are increasingly trading off future opportunity for present experiences. More and more millennials are getting lost in their careers in their late-twenties and early thirties because they didn't use their earlier time to find a targeted goal.

There will come times in your career that you will be offered other positions. Maybe another manager sees your potential and wants you on their team. Or maybe you volunteer for a project and were offered the option to stay on that team, or even lead it. Or maybe another company comes along looking to poach you. Each time an opportunity presents itself, you need to weigh the risks and benefits. Just like everything in life, there is always a compromise to every choice. It comes down to one really simple question: are you taking this position because it is right for your long-term career goals, or because it is a "cool experience?"

Remember my client, Mike Glass? He is the Vice President of Global Talent at a prominent and well-regarded Fortune 100 company, and he told me a story that summarized his concerns. A young woman and a high potential talent who had been working in his organization for two years approached him about a managerial role that had recently opened up. Mike, while supportive, wanted to know more about her personal goals and how it would fit within her career path. Instead of focusing on the management job the young woman was inquiring about, Mike asked about what he called her "destination role." The woman replied that she was ultimately interested in becoming a consultant, and before long, both she and Mike concluded that the only reason why she was seeking the management job was because it was something she didn't have on her résumé. However, a career in consulting is heavily weighted toward being an individual contributor rather than a manager. If this individual took the managerial job, it likely could have been a waste of time (potentially two years). She would have collected an experience that would have little value in terms of her achieving her full potential and personal career aspirations. As Mike would later share with me, "… together, he and this woman created a new plan that helped put her on track toward her desired destination role—she became certified in a variety of tools and approaches, analyzed her chosen market, built an online presence, had her select and join professional organizations, and more."[55]

Don't get me wrong, there is a lot to be said for "cool experiences." But are the compromises you will make when you take that job worth the delay in meeting your primary goal? Making the wrong move can set you back a year, or two, or longer. You have to decide if it's worth the risk. Only you can make that decision, and both are valid choices as long as you go into them with your eyes wide open. However, it is important that if you do decide in favor of the "cool experience," you don't make a habit of it. You don't want to be the person that bounces around.

Years ago, bouncing around from one company to the next was viewed negatively, but now it's not uncommon for people to be in a position anywhere from two to five years before moving on. Today, bouncing around really means changing industries or changing specialties. If you are an IT person and you suddenly decide you want to be in HR, and then you switch to marketing, you're going to struggle to ever make significant progress in your career goals. Some people really do find happiness by making a switch, but you need to weigh every decision against your ultimate goals. This can be really difficult at times. A company could come in and offer you a boatload of money. But if it isn't right for you, is it really worth the money? You may just be trading your cool experience at the expense of your potential.

I know this from personal experience. The same thing also happened to me after college: I got shoehorned into a finance job that wasn't a fit for my aspirations, and I ended up changing gears twice before getting to where I am. I had to assess whether to take the safe road, or risk it all; take a ton of money or do what I love. I made deliberate choices in pursuit of my overall goal, and that is what is important here. This is the most important thing to remember about work experience: it's only useful in the long run if it helps you advance your career. Of course, hindsight is 20/20, and you shouldn't look at work through rose-colored glasses. You have to decide for yourself what kind of risk tolerance you have. The moral of the story here is that you need to be patient and make deliberate and purposeful job rotations and career choices.

BECOME A MENTOR

Earlier, we discussed finding two mentors: an internal mentor within your company, and an external mentor. Hopefully you have those people already and maintain a strong relationship with them both. Once you become more established in your career, it will be time for you to pay it forward. You will still keep your own mentors—that's lifelong—but you'll want to start offering to mentor one or two others as well.

There is a lot of benefit to being a mentor. The altruistic motives are that you are helping someone else in the way others helped you. But let's be honest, these are symbiotic relationships. There is both give and take. Your mentees will also become great connections for you. They can introduce you to new aspects of your company. Or if they move on (or are external mentees), they can provide you connections to other companies, resources, and products. Mentors also show higher levels of job satisfaction than non-mentors and are often rewarded with raises and promotions.[56]

I do want to add a caveat here though. Don't overload yourself. Don't try to help too many people in this capacity. You have limited time and resources, and you need to respect that about yourself. Be selective in who you mentor. Look for people you genuinely think would most benefit from the opportunity to learn from you. Don't just look for someone who is like you. I frequently hear things like "I took him under my wing because I saw a bit of myself in him/her." It's a nice sentiment, but those are probably the people who need your help the least. It will become more of a social hour than a true mentorship relationship.

So how do you go about mentoring someone? It can seem a little daunting at first, but the whole point is to share your expertise and experiences. There are a lot of resources out there on the topic of becoming a mentor, and I encourage you to do some research if you're unsure of how to proceed. Those resources will have all kinds of practical tips. I'm not so concerned with that. You are a highly motivated person and I have every confidence that you will find your own successful path to being a mentor. I just want to address a few of the big-picture elements to mentoring. The three main components are:

1. Making connections.
2. Being supportive.
3. Listening.

Making connections is easy. Be actively aware of opportunities for your mentee. Introduce them to your connections wherever and whenever appropriate. Celebrate their successes and be supportive during the times when they are struggling—at work and in life. Finally, actively listening and empathizing with your mentee is essential. Remember, they may not always have the same experiences or background as you do. It may be more productive to provide emotional support rather than practical support. This means listening rather than problem solving.

As it happens, you'll often hear this issue discussed in regard to couples and marriages,[57] but the advice holds true for pretty much all relationships including that of mentor/mentee. Listening can be a powerful tool. Save the problem solving for when they ask for your advice.

AFFECT CHANGE FROM WITHIN

We all know that nobody and no job is perfect. You may see things that need to change within your company and there will be opportunities for you to do this. This takes a diplomatic and timely approach that will showcase your leadership skills down the road. And how your company handles these issues can tell you a lot about its leadership and corporate values.

First of all, you can't go in blazing for change. Be thoughtful and considerate. Make sure you understand the full scope of the situation before you start making suggestions. When you determine the time is right, thoughtfully approach your leaders with not just an assessment of the problem, but also a solution. There is a lot of discussion right now about DE&I policies. Most companies have them, but they may not be outlined to the detail you want to see. Or the company may not be "living" those policies. This would be an excellent opportunity to form a task force, if one doesn't already exist, to address change. Work for change within the system and programs available. Garner support among your colleagues and the HR team. But also pay attention to the response. If there is high-level resistance to addressing the issue in any form, this may be a big red flag for you at this company.

Another common issue is the concept of "unlimited vacation." Many companies are utilizing this, yet research shows that this policy means employees will actually work *more*, not less.[58] When there is uncertainty in a policy, it can lead to a hesitation to utilize it. Asking for clearly defined rules about how you can utilize policies like this can make not only your own situation better, but also that of all your colleagues and those who follow in your steps. On that note, make sure you are taking vacations. This is one of the most important aspects to avoiding burnout. Furthermore, studies show that vacations and time off actually improve your quality of work.[59] This might lead to other changes, too. Perhaps you can advocate moving to the four-day workweek, which also has advantages. Or maybe you will find other things you want to change. You may not succeed in making those changes, looking to do things better is always a good thing. I'm a big believer in working smarter, not harder.

There are going to be lots of opportunities like these to provide feedback to your leaders. The key is to do this in a respectful, diplomatic, and timely way. I've seen a lot of young people come in and try to force their worldview on a company, and then quit in an explosive manner when they don't get their way. It's embarrassing. And unproductive. That's not to say there won't be an appropriate time to quit if things reach a level of unacceptable behavior or an unwillingness to even discuss the issues you raise. But don't burn bridges if you can help it. There is a time and place for everything.

STAYING THE COURSE

Once you're in the job, it's likely that you will be there for several years. In some cases (like my client Mike Glass) you may stay many years at the same company. Or you may switch companies every five years. Whether you move on or not is determined by a variety of factors: how much job satisfaction you have, promotion and salary increases, geographical location, other benefits like working remotely or having flexible hours, etc. Whatever your path *will* be, for now what you need to focus on is committing to your own success, to your team and company, to your career roadmap, and to yourself.

For now, focus on taking advantage of every offer and opportunity you can. Mentors, educational opportunities, benefits packages (like discounted stock options, and matched investments to your 401K, etc.), new initiative opportunities, and DEFINITELY take advantage of your annual review. The C in #PACE is Commit for a reason. Now is the time to focus on that. We've gone over a ton of tips on how to achieve this, but like everything else in this book, it really comes down to mindset. Staying the course and committing is a true mindset and one you need to have day in and day out. Don't let a bad day or even a bad week or month derail your plan. But work through the bad days and give yourself the time and space for things to get better. If they don't, then perhaps it's time explore new options and we will cover that next in Section 4.

If you're not sure whether you need to reevaluate your current career path, don't be afraid to sit down with your mentor or your supervisor and discuss your future. Have an open and honest conversation with someone you trust about where you're headed and what opportunities will be available to you if you stay on your current track. Weigh the pros and cons in the context of your goals and definition of success. If the cons outweigh the pros, then it may be time to do some hard thinking about what you're looking for, and what you're willing to sacrifice in order to get it. When in doubt, listen to what your gut is telling you. Odds are, it's right.

#PACE PROCESS STEPS

- **Define success.** What does being successful mean to you? Is it work-related? Is it based on a title, a salary, or a lifestyle? Is it based on the impact you want to make on the world? Whatever success looks like to you, define it clearly.
- **Don't be afraid of lateral moves.** This is a journey. Pauses and sidesteps are part of the natural course. Embrace that.
- **Fully utilize your annual review.** Don't skimp on this. Take it seriously and make your manager do so as well. It's scary at times, but the benefits absolutely outweigh the momentary discomfort.
- **Negotiate for what you're worth.** You may not always get it, but if don't ask, you likely never will.
- **Be wary about trading long-term potential for something "cool."** Go into every career opportunity with your eyes open and make a deliberate, thoughtful choice.

- **Become a mentor.** Pay it forward. People are helping you, so you want to help those that follow. It's as good for you as it is for them.
- **Work for internal change.** Don't be afraid to work to change things within if you see opportunities for your company to do better.
- **Stay the course.** Give yourself the right mindset, and the time and space for success in a role. There may come a time when it becomes clear that you need to move on. But don't be too hasty getting there. Commit to doing your best in the moment.

SECTION 4

EVALUATE

#PACE: PREPARE + APPLY + COMMIT + EVALUATE

AT THIS POINT, I really hope you are killing it at your job—making the impact you want, climbing the corporate ladder, and finding all the success you desire. Hopefully you won't need this last section for some time. That said, you can go ahead and read it now. Just keep it in the back of your mind and hold on to this book for reference when you need it. It's here for whenever you're ready to explore your next steps, your next opportunity, or if things go bad and you need to move on. Unfortunately, that happens and you should be prepared for it.

The E in #PACE is for evaluate. You can and should be exploring your options. There is nothing wrong with that, even if you are happy in your current position. You should be open to new opportunities when they come your way. Maybe that's in the form of entrepreneurship. Or maybe it's just moving on to the next company. Or maybe your company goes through a culture change and it's no longer a place where you want to stay. It might not even a place that would be healthy to stay. Obviously, I believe strongly in Committing from Section 3, but taking care of yourself is important, too, as long as you are not doing it over the misguided belief that the world owes you something. That it should all be easy. Things will get tough.

We all go through periods where we dislike our jobs. Sometimes you have to power through and sometimes it's time to move on. Even if things are going really well, it could still be time to move on if there is something else out there that would be even more fulfilling. It's your job to figure out which is which. And that's no easy task. It's also something I can't answer for you. But I can help you consider your options. We're going to talk about some of the questions to ask yourself as you move into this stage of your career.

CHAPTER 10
WHEN YOU NEED TO RECALIBRATE

IT DOESN'T MATTER WHO YOU ARE or what your background is, whether you're just starting out or have launched a billion-dollar company. One thing is universal: the journey to career success is rarely ever straightforward. As we discussed in Section 3, our careers are rarely sequential, where one role or project leads seamlessly to another until we make it to the top, but rather our paths to success are a winding journey, with pauses, sidesteps, and obstacles along the way. This is going to sound contradictory, especially after I just spent a whole chapter talking about roadmaps and checklists, but it's an important discussion to have, and it all comes down to one question. Is your next step aligned with your goals?

CHANGING GEARS

I had three big moments of reckoning during my journey to founding CoreAxis. The first one was after I graduated Babson College, when I found myself going through the motions of a finance job I had no passion for. The second was when my first company, Progressive Solutions, failed to go public. I was on the verge of becoming a millionaire, but the market crash of 2000 threw a major curveball into my plans. That was a watershed moment for me; my wife and I had just had our first child and we knew we needed stability, and I agonized for a long time over whether I needed to give up entrepreneurship altogether. Ultimately, I gave it one more shot and founded CoreAxis, which led to my third big moment of uncertainty.

For eight years after creating CoreAxis, the company didn't have an identity. I managed to keep the lights on by continuing to keep my networks open while also taking full time, more traditional Talent Management Leadership roles at three different companies: Ernst and Young, Monitor Group, and PWC. During this period, I had my second and third child, and though the jobs themselves weren't what I had envisioned for myself, things were going well. Even though these great firms were not where I thought that I would be, things were going incredibly well. I was learning a lot, making a difference to the clients that I served, while building many important business relationships. I was fortunate to have many great mentors, and was able to work with leaders who are luminaries and much smarter than I am. All of these experiences helped me acquire many new perspectives that I did not have earlier in my career. The roles in these companies enabled me to become a better leader while gaining the knowledge of how large, matrix global firms are organized. These seven years were an important building block in my personal journey.

Then came 2008.

The Great Recession brought the world of finance and banking to its knees, and overnight, my job shifted underneath me. I transitioned into working on divestitures, situations where companies were going out of business, in an effort to help PWC save its clients. I was traveling nonstop—five days per week for over six months—and working in an environment where people were losing their livelihoods. That wasn't what I had signed up for.

Things came to a head in November. My next trip brought me to the Wachovia operations center, as people were being forced out of their jobs due to the financial crisis. I was delayed in Chicago, and almost didn't make it back in time for Thanksgiving with my family. The world felt like it had turned upside down in an instant, and my life was getting away from me. Late that night, I sat down with my wife, and we discussed my options. PWC was—and still is—a world-class management firm that impacts lives and businesses every day. But the more I reflected on the transformation I was going through as a young executive, the more I realized that I wanted to create change and relate to people on a more practical level. Continuing down my path at PWC would have meant sacrificing the ability to make my own decisions about how I wanted my work to impact the world. As good as PWC was, the change in the market dictated that I needed to make a move. I wanted to be more flexible and align my work with my personal goals and attributes.

Through these reflections, I realized that life was too short to continue down a road that wasn't for me. I had always been happiest running my own business, and that was what I was determined to do. After really assessing my goals and next steps, asking myself all those hard questions we've discussed, I knew it was time to change gears. The next week, I decided to move on from PWC and threw myself into breathing new life into CoreAxis, restarting CoreAxis as a consulting firm providing custom solutions to the marketplace. This was the worst possible time to attempt to get a business off the ground, and the first nine months were an incredible challenge. Unemployment benefits were difficult to obtain with the high rate of growth our country was seeing, and I had to sell my 401k just to keep things rolling, but I kept my head down and my eyes on the prize, and now business has never been better! My company has had consistent growth and all those risks paid off.

The point here is that you may eventually find yourself at a crossroads in your career—especially with constant advancements with technology, transportation methods, and traditional working environments evolving rapidly. Maybe, like me, you'll find yourself in the midst of a financial crisis. Maybe you'll wake up one day and realize that what you're currently doing isn't what you really *want* to be doing. Maybe you won't even know why you're dissatisfied with your career path but won't be able to shake an overarching sense of uneasiness. Eventually, you might have to decide whether to stay on your current track or change course, and this could very well be one of the most important decisions, if not *the* most important decision, that you make in your career.

LEARNING TO SAY NO EVEN WHEN IT'S SAFER TO SAY YES

By the time I decided to leave PWC in 2008, I was already a principle there (partner level). The executives couldn't understand why I would want to leave, especially when the economy was in shambles and my job there was secure. They offered me a lot of money to stay on, but I still declined. That money would have been huge, and I probably seemed crazy for turning it down with the country in the midst of such an enormous financial crisis. To me, it wasn't about the money. It was about my ability to lead my own company, watch my kids grow up, and feel like I was building something that would add value to society.

Given my circumstances, it would have been easy to shut up, take the money, and keep my job. But what would I have been sacrificing long-term? For one thing, time with my family. By then, I was doing an insane amount of business traveling, and it was more draining on me than I ever would have thought possible. As the father of three young kids, staying where I was would mean sacrificing valuable time with them at a critical period during their lives. There was also my own definition of success. Was I willing to waste more of my time working for someone else in a job that I didn't feel had meaning for me, or was I going to take the plunge and give running a company another shot? It was a choice between discomfort and fear in the present moment and overall disappointment with my career later on in life. That money was momentary, but the ability to look back on my work and not regret the chances I didn't take? That's a satisfaction that will last a lifetime and choosing to pursue it despite the risks was the best thing I could have done for my future self.

Often, when you're at a crossroads, what's easiest and what's best are two very different things. Depending on your situation, you may need to do anything from looking for a new job to completely resetting your career, restarting from the ground up, moving to a different field, or becoming a freelancer. This will probably mean a lot of difficulty in the present. You may be looking at a significant pay cut, having to get additional education, learning a new industry or type of work, or dropping back to the bottom of the corporate ladder. If you know what you want, and you know that you won't get it by staying where you are, then you'll find a way to make it happen.

The gig economy is a perfect example of this. There are many jobs you can do on the side that can help you cover your expenses while you pursue your ideal career trajectory. This isn't easy either. The gig economy can also be very "feast or famine." You'll have to hustle, but it can often be a source of income that will help you get to where you want to go. The other side of the gig economy is that you may be able to utilize it to build up your experience or portfolio in a way that will allow you to get the position you want, work for the company you want, or build up your own portfolio of expertise as you build your company. Definitely something to consider!

Ten years down the line, when you're looking back on your journey, you'll remember the choices you didn't make, so don't set yourself up for regret. It's the best gift you can give yourself.

GIVING YOURSELF PERMISSION TO CHANGE COURSE

Perfectionism is the enemy of growth, because when we spend all our energy on making sure we don't screw up, we're closing ourselves off to the chance to learn. It's another lesson that isn't easy, especially because as adults we don't deal with change as well. We fear judgement and pain and embarrassment. But if we can train ourselves out of that fear, our growth is limitless. Take Elon Musk for example; love him or hate him, you can't deny his success. He has two quotes in particular that apply here. The first is, "When you struggle with a problem, that's when you understand it." This is so true. When we persist in working through something, it sticks with us. We remember it and we understand it far better than if it had been instantaneous. The other quote is, "Failure is an option here. If things are not failing, you are not innovating enough." Think about how little kids navigate challenges. If you watch kids trying to solve a problem, you'll notice that they aren't hung up on getting it right on the first try. They iterate, think outside the box, and when they fail, they laugh it off and try again. They don't put pressure on themselves to succeed every time, and when they fail, they try something different.

When it comes to your career, you'll hit dead ends, and even something that seems to be working at first might not pan out. Our tendency as adults is to pick the devil we know over the devil we don't know. We think *I could try something new, but I don't know if I will succeed. I would rather stick to a job I know I can do, even if it makes me miserable.* It's time to flip the script. Think like a kid. Instead of framing an unsuccessful career move as a failure, think of it as an opportunity to learn what works and what doesn't work. You're now one step closer to getting on the right track. Instead of closing yourself off from risks, give yourself permission to revive that "learning mindset." It's never too late to switch gears, so keep your vision in the forefront, and embrace change instead of fearing it.

Distancing from what—and who—holds you back.

WHEN THE PROBLEM IS A TOXIC WORKPLACE

Like it or not, we're influenced by other people's behavior. Unfortunately, not everyone in life has your best interests at heart, and you may even encounter people who are actively sabotaging you in your pursuit of your goals. This might come from jealousy, insecurity, or a lack of understanding of what you want for yourself. It may stem from a fear of you getting what they can't. People today seem to have this idea that they are owed something. Owed success. Owed respect. Owed whatever they want. And when some people don't get it, they lash out. It often doesn't even have anything to do with you, but rather with their own internal struggles. Keep an eye out for the following behaviors from other people, which are common both in and out of workplace settings:

- **Excessive negativity:** There's a difference between playing the devil's advocate and bringing others down. If someone can't seem to find a constructive way to present their feedback or is only ever interested in pointing out the flaws they perceive in you, they aren't being helpful; they're being petty.
- **Not celebrating your successes:** You can tell a lot about a person by observing how they respond to success that isn't

their own. Is your coworker acting bitter because you kicked ass on a project? Is a friend trying to downplay an award, recognition, or promotion? If the people around you can't seem to be happy for you when you're doing well, then they likely don't have your best interests at heart.

- **Making their problems your problems:** This is especially important with coworkers. You may find yourself dealing with someone who likes to project their own stress and insecurities onto the people around them, and if you're tuned in to others' emotions, this may leave you feeling drained and beaten down. When you're spending all your cycles absorbing other people's issues, you're left without the energy you need to address your own.

- **Taking advantage of you:** Be on the lookout for people who always seem to want things from you, but are never there when you need things from them. If someone consistently asks for favors but can never be bothered to give you a hand once in a while, they might just be capitalizing on your skills. Interpersonal relationships are supposed to be a give-and-take dynamic, not all give and no take.

If you become aware of people in your life who are dragging you down, you may consider putting some distance between them and yourself. This is easier said than done, so another option is to steer clear of discussing your work and success with them. It's important to remember that you don't need to be everybody's friend. It's okay to be polite and professional colleagues. It's okay to be friendly acquaintances. And it's okay to keep your distance from someone if they are detrimental to your success or wellbeing. Sometimes all it takes is an awareness of when someone isn't benefiting your productivity in order to distance yourself from their negativity. Remember, your success is your business, no one else's.

You may be one of the lucky ones whose road to success progresses predictably and without obstacles, but chances are, you'll find yourself needing to recalibrate at least once or twice in your career. That's the nature of working in a world that changes as rapidly as ours. When you face a big decision, whether to stick around or change jobs, to pursue a new opportunity, or even start from scratch, it's important to return to what success means to you. Ask yourself whether the path you're on is still taking you in that direction, and if it's not, then don't be afraid to take a new road with your eyes wide open.

SOMETIMES THE PROBLEM MIGHT BE YOU

If you sense that something isn't working for you in your career, but you can't put your finger on what it is, the problem might not be external, but internal. You could feel like you've hit a roadblock because you keep being passed over for that promotion, or you aren't innovating as much as the people around you. Maybe you're sure you're on the right track, but you can't seem to move forward no matter what you do. Look for these common self-sabotaging behaviors.

- **Sitting on your laurels:** You're welcome to do the bare minimum of work needed to keep your job, but that's not going to help you progress. If you really want to get noticed and earn respect, you need to show others how you can help them. Look for opportunities to assist others and contribute, even when you don't have to. When in doubt, ask where else you can be of assistance. If you sit around twiddling your thumbs and waiting for your next assignment, you're being reactive, not proactive.

- **Expecting success to be handed to you:** If you're tackling work from a place of entitlement, you're doing it wrong. It's easy to think that climbing the ladder is as simple as showing up every day, but it's not. You have to have a game plan, and you have to be willing to put in the work to make it happen.

- **Not keeping an open mind:** Sometimes, the way forward isn't what we expect. Your supervisor might ask you to try your hand at something new or work in a department you're not familiar with. Take 2020 and 2021 as an example: Employees of all kinds were asked to work in new ways and take on new tasks. If you only focus on what you're comfortable with and good at, you're closing yourself off to areas that might be full of opportunity. Be curious and willing to learn, even if you aren't an immediate expert.

- **Not accepting feedback.** Listen to the critiques your colleagues give you. You may not always agree, but you should at least consider their viewpoint. Take notes during performance reviews, and pay attention to criticism whenever it comes up, even if it's unpleasant. The way to show you're ready for the next step isn't just to be qualified. It's to prove that you can not only hear feedback, but also synthesize it and incorporate it into your work style.

- **Not asking for that promotion:** If you feel you're ready for the next level, make that known to your superiors. You would be surprised how many people are promoted just because they had the guts to ask. That said, even if the answer is "no," that doesn't mean "never," so if you don't get it on the first try, ask what you can do to improve your chances. This is a great way to calibrate your strategy to land the next role you have your eyes on.

Don't be afraid to seek out some tough love from the people around you. Ask your supervisor why, in their opinion, you're not making progress, and pay careful attention to the reasons they give. If they point to issues with your performance or work style, then you know what to address moving forward. *Address it.* If your behavior is preventing you from advancing, then work on changing your habits and mindset. This will take time and work, but when success is on the line, it's worth every effort.

On the other hand, if they make excuses or can't give you a concrete answer, that's a red flag, and a sign that the issue might not be with you after all.

THE WARNING SIGNS OF BURNOUT

Burnout is real, and it's a problem. Burnout is at an all-time high right now. Remote work is certainly a piece of this problem. Sometimes people feel isolated working in this manner. There is also the stress of the pandemic. And the fact that companies are relying on current employees to cover labor shortages in other departments. This can all cause a lot of stress. But you're no use to anyone—least of all yourself—if you push yourself to the breaking point. Be aware of how you're handling your responsibilities, and watch out for these telltale signs of burnout as described by *Psychology Today*:

1. "Chronic fatigue. In the early stages, you may feel a lack of energy and feel tired most days. In the latter stages, you feel physically and emotionally exhausted, drained, and depleted, and you may feel a sense of dread about what lies ahead on any given day.

2. Insomnia. In the early stages, you may have trouble falling asleep or staying asleep one or two nights a week. In the latter stages, insomnia may turn into a persistent, nightly ordeal; as exhausted as you are, you can't sleep.

3. Forgetfulness/impaired concentration and attention. Lack of focus and mild forgetfulness are early signs. Later, the problems may get to the point where you can't get your work done and everything begins to pile up.

4. Physical symptoms. Physical symptoms may include chest pain, heart palpitations, shortness of breath, gastrointestinal pain, dizziness, fainting, and/or headaches (all of which should be medically assessed).

5. Increased illness. Because your body is depleted, your immune system becomes weakened, making you more vulnerable to infections, colds, flu, and other immune-related medical problems.

6. Loss of appetite. In the early stages, you may not feel hungry and may skip a few meals. In the latter stages, you may lose your appetite altogether and begin to lose a significant amount of weight.

7. Anxiety. Early on, you may experience mild symptoms of tension, worry, and edginess. As you move closer to burnout, the anxiety may become so serious that it interferes with your ability to work productively and may cause problems in your personal life.

8. Depression. In the early stages, you may feel mildly sad and occasionally hopeless, and you may experience feelings of guilt and worthlessness as a result. At its worst, you may feel trapped and severely depressed and think the world would be better off without you. (If your depression is to this point, you should seek professional help immediately.)

9. Anger. At first, this may present as interpersonal tension and irritability. In the latter stages, this may turn into

angry outbursts and serious arguments at home and in the workplace. (If anger gets to the point where it turns to thoughts or acts of violence toward family or coworkers, seek immediate professional assistance.)"[60]

There can be many causes of burnout. External factors can certainly play a role, but we are going to focus on the ones that are most common in the workplace. These can include unrealistic work expectations, micromanagement, poor instruction, isolation (one of the bigger ones right now), and lack of support and unfair treatment.[61] Unfortunately, all of these will likely happen to you at some point in your career. But if you are aware of them, you can address them when the first arise, *before* they become a problem. There is nothing wrong with you if you seek help—we are all only human.

This can also be something that can inspire exploring the job market again. Let's say you get a new supervisor. There is a minor hiccup during the transition from the old supervisor to the new one. The new supervisor decides to suddenly start micromanaging your every move, despite you consistently performing above expectations apart from that one hiccup. It creates an environment of stress. What you do you next, and what your company does, can tell you a lot.

If you request help from HR, from your supervisor, or from his/her supervisor and you receive it, then you have resources available to help you work through it. You can find solutions to avoid burnout. But first you have to be brave enough to ask. It may not be easy, but it is necessary if you are going to progress onward to your goal. It might still be good to explore your options to see if there is a lateral move you can make to reduce your stress, or other options available to you within the company or outside it. This will hopefully allow you to start the process to finding balance.

So how do you find balance between avoiding burnout and always pushing to achieve? It's simple: figure out where your limits are, and then operate a bit under it—not too far, but enough that you can sustainably keep your pace. This will take some trial and error because everyone is different. See how you do at 90 percent. If it feels like you could do a little more after that, try 95 percent. If you need to take another step back, try 80 percent. Start working to find your own personalized solution for balance.

But if you request help, and you don't receive it, then that is a major red flag. Your company is not going to support you and the problem will only get worse. Sophie Theen, an HR and DE&I expert advises this: "You will need to create governance for yourself, then create boundaries for yourself, because if your manager is expecting you to work until 11:00 p.m., that's a problem. Even if it's not necessarily physically working, but just sending you an email at 11:00 p.m. and expecting you to respond immediately, that eats into your personal time. That's not working your core hours." It's those unreasonable expectations that lead to burnout. You have to advocate for yourself. And if nothing changes, you need to start exploring new positions immediately and consider leaving that company behind. You may not have the option to do this immediately. We all have bills to pay. But the moment you can safely exit, you should.

Remember, keeping the #Pace isn't about things always being easy. The point is to find a sweet spot: *What's the most that I can do without overdoing it?* This will change over time as you move from role to role and navigate life outside your career. If something major happens in your personal life, you might not be able to push as hard as you would have otherwise. Then again, if things have been smooth sailing for a while, there's no harm in testing the waters to see if you can put in a little extra time and effort.

WHEN & HOW TO MOVE ON

If it is time to move on, it's really important that you do it the right way. We've discussed personal brand a lot throughout this book. How you leave a company will play into your brand, I assure you. No matter what industry you are in, it is a much smaller, more insular world than you think it is. People talk. You want them talking about the right thing, not how you left your last company in a blaze of 'glory.'

Once you've made your decision, your first step should be to put in your notice. Remember when I insisted you read your contract? You need to know what kind of notice your company expects. Two weeks is commonplace, but it's not unheard of for you to be required to give one month's notice. Whatever the requirement, put in the appropriate notice. It is considered a courtesy to notify your boss before anyone else. Then consult with HR and finally, you should notify your team.

At this time, HR will likely help you develop an exit plan. This will entail handing off your projects to other employees, making sure your work is backed up on the company servers, filling out the appropriate paperwork, and returning any company property. It will also likely entail the "Exit Interview." This is an opportunity for the company to find out why you are leaving.

There are two schools of thought. One is to be professional but honest. The other is to keep your mouth shut. The first has the benefit of potentially making things better for those who follow in your former position. But companies often take that information badly, no matter how professionally and politely you deliver it. It could also ruin any chance to work for the company again or receive positive referrals and could impact working with those same employees at a future company. It's a risk, so the safer course is to just say you found an exciting new opportunity and decided to take it. Leave it at that.

Whatever you do, do not get emotional. Don't list every complaint and problem you had with the company, your bosses, or your colleagues. It will follow you, and it will affect your personal brand. No one wants to work for someone who bashes everyone else on their way out.

You may ask, well if I already have a new job lined up, what's the harm? You might even be right… for now. But what about the next job. Or the next one? Don't be hasty. Keep it professional. This really should be your mantra throughout your career. With every decision, every option, every situation, do your utmost to keep it polite and keep it professional.

#PACE PROCESS STEPS

- **Consider where you are now.** Is your current job still leading you to where you want to be years from now? Is there still room for growth? Does your job still mesh with your values and life plan? Remember, the problems you're having could be temporary or intrinsic, so figure out which they are before hitting the brakes. Sometimes a few adjustments are all that is required.
- **Saying "yes" isn't always the right answer.** It may be easier to stay where you are, but if your long-term happiness depends on making a change, take the plunge. Don't wait until you're regretting the paths you didn't take.
- **Take risks and be open to new possibilities.** Approach obstacles like a kid. View false starts and dead ends through a lens of learning and experimentation, not failure and

stagnation. What you thought you wanted when you first started out might not be what you want now.

- **Watch for warning signs of burnout.** Don't be afraid to get the help you need. This is really essential. If you allow yourself to burn out, you will never be able to achieve all you desire.
- **Identify what's holding you back.** Consult with others to identify flaws in your work style and commit to fixing them. If the issue is the negative attitudes of the people around you, find a way to distance yourself.
- **Exit gracefully.** Follow proper procedures and keep it professional. Maintain those work relationships and preserve your personal brand as you leave your position.

CHAPTER 11
YOUR PASSIONS

IN CHAPTER 10, I told you the story of my own path to entrepreneurship. For me, it was the right move. It was time for me to change gears, and I was not only following my passion, but also my ultimate career roadmap. Maybe this will be a part of your own journey. Maybe it won't. This chapter is all about how to decide for yourself.

IS ENTREPRENEURSHIP FOR YOU?

Entrepreneurship is a big buzz word right now. It's easy to understand why. Who doesn't dream of being their own boss? In fact, the majority of Americans do.[62] But is it really something you should do? Are you really prepared for all that it entails and all the risks? Don't get me wrong, there are a lot of benefits. I don't want to discourage you. But I do want to provide a reality check. It's not easy, and it's not for everyone. Don't do it just because it's trendy.

There is a great article in *Inc.* that has the best list of signs you are ready.[63] But I prefer to think of these as questions. In fact, I recommend you buy a journal and give each question careful thought and consideration. Sometimes writing it out can help you think things through, and it can also make it more real.

1. Do you daydream about being your own boss?
2. Do you *know*, deep down, that you have what it takes?
3. Do you dream of something *better*?
4. Have you already started making connections in this field?
5. Are you obsessed about learning more about the field and about what it will take to make the change into owning your own business?
6. Are you tired of putting your efforts into someone else's dream?
7. Are you passionate about putting every spare moment into realizing your dream?

And I'd also add a few more.

8. Does this idea excite you, at least as much as it scares you?
9. Are you ready to make a real, practical plan and are you prepared for the not so fun parts? Taxes, payroll, legalese, etc.?
10. Do you have the support of your people? Spouse, kids, etc. This impacts them as well.

When you've directly and honestly addressed these questions, if your answers are yes then *MAKE THE MOVE!* Congratulations! You're an entrepreneur. The world awaits your genius. The cool thing is that remote work and hybrid work have really opened up a lot of options for you as an entrepreneur. Ones that didn't exist when I was getting started. But make sure that when you make this change you still go back to that career map and adjust it. Manage your expectations for your true goals. Do you want to be the next billionaire like Elon Musk and Jeff Bezos? Or are you more concerned with the impact you will make? Perhaps you want something that allows you to spend more time with your family, or to travel more (or both). Define what you want and work toward it.

FOLLOWING YOUR PASSIONS

You've determined that you are ready to make the move to entrepreneurship. I assume you have your product or service pretty much figured out at this point. If you don't have at least some idea, stop now and figure that out. Then come back to this.

Assuming from here on out that you do have your plan in place, let's talk a bit about following your passion. While you may know what your business is going to do, what you're going to sell, and maybe even how you're going to sell it, I bet you don't really know what *you're* going to do. Sure, at first you're probably going to be doing it all unless you have the investments to hire staff right away. But once you grow beyond the one-man-shop stage, you will really need to focus on where you fit into the picture. I bet you're thinking, "Well, I'll be CEO of course." Maybe you will. But is that where your skills really fit? Is that really what you enjoy doing on a daily basis?

Brad Johnson's wisdom has appeared several times in this book, and here is another gem. As he puts it, "There are three major categories of roles: subject matter expertise, project management, and people management." As the founder, you will have subject matter expertise. You will know your product or service better than anyone. That may eventually change as you expand out to offering many products and hiring many employees. Then there is project management and people management considerations. Which one do you really love? It's likely you will do one of these two. Are you good at getting people where they need to be? Good at assembling the right team for the job and dealing with the issues that arise? Or are you better at strategizing and building the project and then handing it off later to someone else to manage? For the record, by Brad's own admission, he's the latter. He loves to build things, and he's really, really good at it. But he has no desire to be in charge after that. He'd rather go build the next big thing.

That's what following your passion really means. It's not just building your company, or expanding it, or doing any of those big things. It's about finding the skills and tasks that fulfill you. Don't be afraid to hire others to take on the tasks you don't want to do. Follow your passion and your own skills.

ALTERNATIVE COURSES

Let's be honest. A lot of you read those questions at the beginning of this chapter, and went… well, nope! That's okay. It's not for everyone. Maybe you will stick with your corporate path. But I do want to broach that there may be other options for you, too.

- **Partnerships:** Just because you answered "No" to some of those questions doesn't mean entrepreneurship is out of the question. Maybe it's just a "not yet," or "not right now." Maybe you just need the right partnership. Assembling the right team to join you on this journey could be exactly what you need. There are trade-offs (Like Mike Glass said earlier, there are *always* trade-offs.)
- **Invest:** Have you saved up some money? Then perhaps you can invest in someone else's endeavor. Find something you believe in and be a silent partner. Or a venture capitalist. You'd be surprised what people can do with even small sums of money.
- **Move to a start up.** If you've worked your entire career in a very large, stable company, maybe you should look into finding a new challenge. If you are stable and able to take

the pay cut, maybe working for a start-up is the challenge you need. All of the fun, less of a risk. It's not your name, your money, or your idea on the line. But it will present new challenges and could be the right fit for you.

The real moral of the entrepreneurship journey is do what's right for *you*. There are lots of options out there.

#PACE PROCESS STEPS

- **Consider the real questions about entrepreneurship.** Don't jump in without sincerely contemplating these questions. You'll regret it if you do. Be deliberate.
- **Be honest with yourself.** Don't fall into something just because it's cool or trendy. Honest self-assessment is key.
- **Make a plan.** How does remote work or hybrid work fit into your plan? Do you have a formal business plan? Figure out the practical as soon as possible.
- **Follow your passions *and* your skills.** When the time is right, do what you do best. Hire others to fill the gaps.
- **Don't discount the alternatives.** Find the right fit for *you*.

CHAPTER 12
KEEPING #PACE

MY GOAL IN WRITING THIS BOOK was to give you useful guidance for getting started on the path to career success. In Section 3 and earlier in this last section, I talked about what happens when you hit a bump in the road, but what about when things are going well? When you have a clear idea of your career goals and how to get there, how do you ensure you're getting the most out of your journey? When you know you're on the right track, how do you make sure you stay that way?

KEEPING #PACE

In the prologue, I discussed the idea of #Pace as a process and of *pace* as a lifestyle, and how it's been one of my primary guiding principles throughout my career. Here, I want to dive into it more deeply.

The word "pace" has multiple connotations. In this book, we've defined it as #PACE: Prepare, Apply, Commit, Evaluate. There are other connotations, too. *Keeping the pace,* for example. *Pace yourself—* that's another one. *Outpacing the competition.* #PACE is all of these things and more. It's a mindset. It's a lifestyle. It's a program for success—a way of holding yourself accountable for your own success. When you're keeping the #Pace, you have your finger on the pulse of your career at all times—past, present, and future. You're staying in tune with what your career needs at any given moment, while constantly making small changes to make sure you're always in a sustainable state of growth.

In car racing, the winning driver is the driver that's always at the front, making micro adjustments to make sure that he keeps the lead without derailing. He's the driver everyone else wants to be, and he sets the pace for the race. He doesn't wait for permission from the other drivers to take the lead. He doesn't limit himself to meeting previous records. He moves from moment to moment, never taking his foot off the gas but at the same time never getting complacent with his lead. He knows that if he gets too comfortable, one of the other drivers will speed past him.

Simply put, you set the #Pace of your own life. How quickly do you want to succeed? Are you going to be the driver everyone envies, or the driver everyone pities? How do you make sure you're constantly advancing? What deadlines and objectives have you set for yourself? What's your strategy for getting there?

One thing you need to know about #Pace is that it isn't for people who aren't sure of themselves. You shouldn't be thinking about #Pace when you aren't certain you're on the right track, and you certainly shouldn't be thinking about it when you're having serious doubts about the direction you've chosen. If you haven't figured out what you truly want to do and how to get there, #Pace won't allow you the time to properly think things over. If you're having doubts or encountering issues, focus on sorting them out first, using the techniques I've outlined previously. Only when you're sure that you're on the right track should you work on getting into a #Pace mindset.

FINDING YOUR #PACE

Once you've found the career path you know you want, get to work and don't let up. It's easy to dismiss career milestones, like promotions, accolades, or pay raises, especially when you're early in your career. *That's ten years down the line,* you might think. *I don't really have to worry about that just yet, right?* Wrong.

Thinking about your success as something ethereal, perpetually on the horizon, and not worth worrying about right now is a one-way ticket to a mediocre career. Your success comes directly from what you do *right now.* You're already living your job one way or another; the question is, are you living it with a mindset of growth?

The key to #Pace is acting as if the next opportunity for advancement is always just around the corner. It's to live your life and navigate your career as if tomorrow is the day you'll be considered for that promotion, that salary bump, that award. When you're keeping #Pace, it becomes, "Live each day like it's your last chance to find success."

Take a long look at what you want from your career, using any of the strategies discussed so far (visualizing yourself in the future, using your career roadmap, or evaluating your own definition of success), and then go one step further: *What's the fastest I can go to get where I want to be? What's the hardest I can push myself?* Sometimes, you'll need to ask yourself some tough questions about your own personal definition of success.

Think about the list of career role models you made in Chapter 2. If you want to be like them, you can't sit on your laurels. You must constantly be pushing for the next big thing, and making changes to the way you're used to working when you need to. Can you discuss that promotion now, instead of six months from now? Can you publish that paper, get funding for that project, or ask for that raise today? If that isn't currently possible, what can you do right now to make it possible? Go back to that hustling mindset and kick it into overdrive. That's what makes the difference between meeting your goals this year and meeting them three to five years from now.

Other people might not understand this ambitious, proactive mindset. They're probably thinking in terms of going through the motions and expecting success to come when it feels like it. They might look at you like you're crazy, tell you that you're going too fast, or even try to steer you in a new direction. Most people are comfortable accepting their lot in life without questioning whether there's something better for them out there. Ignore them. These are the people you'll be leaving in the dust. The most important thing about #Pace is that it's unique to you, and it doesn't depend on anyone else. Your own strategy is the only one that matters.

#PACE YOURSELF

I can already hear what you're thinking. *Mark, you can't be serious. That isn't sustainable. If I'm constantly in overdrive, I'm going to burn out.* And you're right. The racecar driver that guns the engine without watching the road will spin out. This is where the second part of the #Pace mentality comes in.

#Pace isn't about always operating at 110 percent. It's about operating at the highest level of performance that's *sustainable* and *achievable* for you at any given time. That level is bound to fluctuate over the months and years, and that's okay. This is where that lovely sentiment of work-life balance comes in. That term gets bandied about a lot now. It's a great concept. But remember the key word is *balance.* You can't let one take over the other. You have to stay on top of your career map *and* keep tabs on your mental health and personal happiness; if you overexert yourself, you'll have to stop sooner or later. Keep *your* pace.

LOOKING TO THE FUTURE

The future of work is something that's getting a lot of airtime these days, usually with a lot of hand-wringing to go with it. In this rapidly-changing landscape, we're going to be hearing even more about sweeping changes that affect the way we work and the kinds of work we do. COVID-19 has brought about a new age of work-from-home and hybrid work environments, and as automation continues to expand, jobs are going to disappear. Odds are, the way we work today is vastly different from the way we will work years into the future. Some roles may not exist anymore, and our current idea of any given career may not look anything like it does a decade from now.

This is a scary concept. With technological advancements speeding up, it's easy to freak out about what this means for your job plans, especially when you're already knee-deep in your career. But there's good news, too: you can future-proof your career, and you don't have to wait for the world to move on without you. Here are some things to work on throughout your career as the future of work continues to change:

- **Prepare for a skills-based economy.** Previously, I discussed planning ahead for when life throws unexpected challenges your way. One of the biggest favors you can do for your future self is to stay on top of your skills. A skills-based economy is the future, and I'm not talking about niche skills, either. Some of the most sought-after abilities are the broad ones, like digital acumen, learning agility, and leadership. I'm not saying you need to ditch your current job altogether but consider finding ways in your current role to get experience in these important areas. How can you take on more leadership and responsibility where you are now? Can you get some extra practice working with and

interpreting data? Find ways of tailoring your role, whatever
it is, to *broad, far-reaching skills.* If you spend too much time
honing a niche ability, you may be in for a rude surprise if it
becomes obsolete farther down the line.

Consider also that there are certain jobs that will never
become irrelevant. We will always need healthcare and
service workers, trade workers (such as plumbers, welders,
and electricians), and engineers, because these industries
are what keep society functioning at a base level. If you're
looking for a backup plan that keeps you employable,
consider starting with one of these "recession proof"
professions. This isn't me telling you to go back to school
and become an engineer, but if you want to expand your
expertise in a way that shores you up against economic
troubles, think about how you might apply your skills to
these areas.

- **Don't just embrace technology. Master it.** Technology
is the way of the future, and it will inevitably touch every
industry out there. There are two ways of approaching
this: putting your head in the sand and pretending it's not
coming, or taking the bull by the horns and learning how to
capitalize on advancements in tech. This doesn't necessarily
mean taking programming classes, but it does mean giving
some hard thought to how your industry could be affected
by things like artificial intelligence, machine learning,
remote work, and e-commerce.

  You may need to think outside the box, but it all comes
down to one question: *How can technology be used to make my
industry more profitable, and what role can I play in making
it happen?* That's the same question the people driving

your field are asking themselves right now and learning
to anticipate shifts in your market based on tech will help
you keep yourself relevant. You have the built-in advantage
of having grown up immersed in technology, so use that
to your benefit. Don't hold yourself to today's business
model because it might not be relevant anymore in five or
ten years.

- **Live with a learning mindset.** Change is inevitable, so
embrace it rather than resisting it. Approach your career
with curiosity and a willingness to re-evaluate your methods
and technological expertise. Stay on top of current events
in your industry, and find opportunities to exchange big-
picture ideas with others. If a new standard, practice, or
innovation comes along that's relevant to your field, read up
on it and ask yourself whether it's something you can utilize.
Above all, don't ever close yourself off to new experiences
and learning opportunities.

- **Keep tabs on your accomplishments.** Specifically, keep
tabs on accomplishments that demonstrate long-term value.
Promotions are just the tip of the iceberg. Innovations and
creative problem-solving are what future employers will
be looking for in a changing industry, so make notes of
these kinds of successes as you move from one role to the
next. Keep track of what you're working on as you work on
it, and ask yourself what skills you've honed or developed
during any given assignment. If you're not currently doing
something that allows you to show off your expertise,
look outside the workplace to courses, classes, professional
certifications, publications, and industry awards. While
actively keeping tabs on your accomplishments, always keep

your résumé, *LinkedIn*, and other career-related profiles current. Even if you're not searching for a new job at the time, it's always smart to let the workforce know what you're capable of and your recent projects/accomplishments/duties.

Regardless of what the future looks like, your top priority is to keep yourself relevant. This is where #Pace comes back in; don't just concern yourself with doing the bare minimum to succeed in the present. Always be on the lookout for opportunities to learn, grow, and challenge yourself, because the work you do now is what will set you apart from your peers.

The key to accomplishment is to stay on your toes, stay relevant, and not get lulled into a false sense of security. By holding yourself accountable for your achievements and always striving for your maximum sustainable output, you'll reach your goals more quickly and efficiently.

Always stay one step ahead. Keep your #Pace.

#PACE PROCESS STEPS

- **Commit to going after what you want.** You always have a choice: stagnation or progress, the easy way or the worthwhile way. Make a conscious decision to keep your goals at the forefront of your mind and do what it takes to make them happen.
- **Future-proof yourself.** Stay on top of technological developments that are relevant to your field. Prepare for change and embrace the unknown with curiosity and flexibility. Keep track of your accomplishments and catalog your projects, whether inside or outside of the workplace. Look for ways to hone broad skills, such as technological fluency, data interpretation, leadership, and communication in your current role.

CONCLUSION

I SINCERELY HOPE THAT THIS BOOK has been useful to you, and that you are able to put these instructions into practice as you launch your career. When I decided to write this, I knew I wanted to pass on what I've learned over the course of my own career to people who may need help starting their own. The way I view work and life, especially when the going gets tough, is the most important thing I can possibly give you.

The thing is, it hasn't been a straightforward path for me. It usually isn't straightforward for anyone else either and that's especially true for today's youngest workers. Maybe you are—or are soon to be—a recent graduate, or maybe you've opted out of school altogether to carve your own path. Whatever your situation, you face a unique set of circumstances. The world is getting smaller, and the competition for jobs is fierce. The prevailing mentality has shifted away from one of *grit* and *determination*, and those are the traits you need most to find success. There are some tough questions you'll have to ask yourself: Are you going to wait for an opportunity to come to you, or are you going to go out and look for it? Are you going to move through your career without a sense of direction, or are you going to make a game plan? Are you going to put in 50 percent or 100 percent?

What I've realized during the course of writing this is that I can't answer those questions for you. You may read them and think, *Okay, this guy is trying to pump me up. He wants me to come away from this motivated and ready to take on the world.* But no matter what words I put on paper here, I can only lay the path out for you. Ultimately, you're the one who has to take the first step. When you're beginning something as long and unpredictable as your career, that first step can feel damn near impossible. Even after reading this, you might not be sure how you'll get from where you are to where you want to be, especially with such an intimidating process ahead of you. The best advice I can give you is to focus on *today*.

I don't mean you shouldn't think about the future—that kind of defeats the purpose of this book—but rather to keep the future in mind *as you concentrate on the present.* What's the most you can do in the next twenty-four hours to put you closer to your goal? What about in the next hour? The next minute? Ask yourself the same thing tomorrow, and then the next day, and then the next day. Tackle what you can in the present and see where it gets you. Whether that's polishing your résumé, putting a few minutes into your career map, or tuning up your network, find the place where you can put in the work right now. Rinse and repeat. That's #Pace. That's what it means to put one foot in front of the other, and it's the way you get to the finish line.

You're going to have doubts. Even if on paper you're doing what you need to, there may be times when you feel like a fraud, like you're just stumbling down the road without knowing if you're doing it right. But that's the secret to adulthood: we all feel that way. God knows I've felt that way more times than I can count. Nobody starts out knowing exactly what they're doing—I think that's a universal part of growing up. But the difference between the dreamers and the achievers is that the achievers don't let those doubts screw with their heads. They push through, and when they find that something isn't working for them, they aren't afraid to adjust their approach and try again. I did this multiple times on my way to where I am, and you will, too—so don't be afraid of those false starts. Embrace them. Listen to what they tell you, internalize it, and use it to put yourself closer to your goal the next time.

There's this expression, *Experience is the best teacher.* So let it teach you. If you only get one thing out of reading this book, I sincerely hope that's it. This habit of giving up every time you fail, of throwing your hands up whenever the going gets tough, kills more dreams than failure ever will. What people don't realize is that dead ends aren't really dead ends; they're really a chance to see that what you're doing isn't working, figure out why, find a new way of attacking the problem, and forging a new path forward.

Don't let failure strike you down. When life throws you a curveball, you're allowed to be upset, but don't use it as a reason not to go after what you want. That's the most important skill you can have in the workplace, and it's one that can't be taught in any lecture or seminar. You have to learn it yourself and really believe it. The rest is white noise.

"I am not concerned that you have fallen—I am concerned that you arise."
— Abraham Lincoln

ACKNOWLEDGMENTS

I HAVE BEEN VERY FORTUNATE throughout my life to grow, work, and create incredible experiences with incredible people. People who bring purpose to my life, challenge me, motivate me, and who are more talented than I am. This book is a combination of much of the wisdom, experiences, and life lessons from all of these important people, who have inspired me to write this book. This is why you are reading this book and why I have so many people to thank.

To my mother, Shirley, and my father Harvey, thank you for the values you instilled in me. I still live by them today. Dad, thank you for pushing me to work hard, study hard, and follow my dreams. You, having an incredible work ethic and being incredibly loyal working at the same company for over thirty-five years, inspired me to work tirelessly to provide for my family when Rachel and I started ours. Mom, I inherited your drive to never give up, to always do my best, and to be passionate about everything I do.

To Mitch; as you know, there are parts of this book that reflect many of the conversations we have had over the years. I appreciate you and am lucky to call you my brother.

To Kimberly Peticolas and Maryann Karinch, who have been great mentors, advisors, and helped me over many hours bringing this book to fruition. You're both talented editors and writers and have incredible knowledge of the book publishing industry. Thank you all for your patience, designs, coaching, inspiration, and energy working with me on this project.

To Mike and Joe, my closest friends, clients, business partners, and advisors, you both have always inspired me to think bigger. Thank you for encouraging me to write this book. I truly enjoy living life to the fullest and sharing so many of those experiences with you.

To Alan Osetek, a co-founder at Recipi, thank you for your loyalty, friendship, daily collaboration, and for showing me how to have fun, while having an honest and equitable partnership.

To the Babson Boys for always being there, believing in me, and having a ton of fun along that way… always keeping the #PACE.

To my friends: the Mancation Crew, thanks to whom I have learned and experienced so much over the years. You guys have made the journey a lot of fun and helped shape my life in such a positive way. A special thank you to Jim Coghlin, who I am lucky enough to call one of my best friends and who always inspires me to work hard and play hard. And the B-R boys, who helped shape me from "unsung" all the way to writing this book and incorporating many of our experiences together over the years.

To many of the contributors to the book, I owe an enormous amount of gratitude. A huge thanks to Mike Glass, Brad Johnson, Jennifer Tice, Alan Walker, Sophie Theen, Scott Johnson, and Zach Frazier. Many of your contributions have found their way onto these pages.

To Erica and Kristie, thank you for always having my back, for making my work life easier, and for helping me free up the time and space to write this book. Your dedication to building CoreAxis with me is a journey that I have enjoyed immensely. We would not be here without you or the incredible teams that you have built over the years. You are truly both a pleasure to work with.

To Terah, Josh, Dudu, Caitlin, Caroline, Fauzia, and Amber (and your teams), you may not recognize yourselves in this book, but your time, energy, and ideas drove many of the impactful pieces. Thank you for being such a big part of our success at CoreAxis and this book launch.

To Isabella, thank you for working with me tirelessly from the inception of the book, taking an early draft of this project and reorganizing the concepts into a structure that is easy to follow and implement. Your style, coaching, collaboration, and creativity are incredible. I am truly grateful.

To my business mentors and colleagues over the years, I appreciate your direct and indirect advice. Much of your feedback inspired me to write this book with the goal of making an impact on the next generation.

To my clients, thank you for the privilege of working with you all over the years and for allowing me to share your stories in this book. What I have learned from all of you is one of my greatest gifts.

For the next generation, this book is really about and for you. All of the experiences coaching, mentoring, and watching many of you over the years drove me to write this book. I cannot wait to watch you all grow, learn, develop, and thrive for many years to come.

To my beautiful wife, Rachel, who inspires me every day and supports me in everything I do, and has been a lifelong partner who makes life fun and meaningful. Finally, to our kids, Zach, Halle, and Keira. You guys are the best! Sarah and Nate, too. I love our #LATEAM. Thank you for all that you do for each other—as a family. I am truly blessed to be part of such an incredible team. I am one lucky guy!

ABOUT THE AUTHOR

MARK IS THE FOUNDER AND CEO of CoreAxis Consulting, an award-winning Learning & Development and Talent Management firm. He is also the founder of Katama, an agency specializing in sales strategy, marketing, and customer success for small-to-medium sized businesses. Over his 30 years advising clients on building future leaders and talent for organizations of all sizes, Mark brings a thoughtful and impactful coaching model to many aspiring trailblazers. He lives in Boston with his wife, three kids, and two labradoodles.

ENDNOTES

1   Peter Economy, "The (Millennial) Workplace of the Future Is Almost Here -- These 3 Things Are About to Change Big Time," Inc. com (Inc., January 15, 2019), https://www.inc.com/peter-economy/the-millennial-workplace-of-future-is-almost-here-these-3-things-are-about-to-change-big-time.html.

2   Joe McKendrick, "Remote Work Evolves Into Hybrid Work And Productivity Rises, The Data Shows," Forbes (Forbes Magazine, June 16, 2021), https://www.forbes.com/sites/joemckendrick/2021/05/30/remote-work-evolves-into-hybrid-work-and-productivity-rises-the-data-shows/?sh=30d1820f4825.

3   "Accenture Strategy Workforce GenZ Class of 2017," Accenture.com, May 5, 2017, https://www.accenture.com/t20170503t022523z__w__/us-en/_acnmedia/pdf-50/accenture-strategy-workforce-genz-class-of-2017-infographic.pdf.

4   Ibid.

5   Jeremy Bauer-Wolf, "Overconfident Students, Dubious Employers," Inside Higher Ed, February 23, 2018, https://www.insidehighered.com/news/2018/02/23/study-students-believe-they-are-prepared-workplace-employers-disagree.

6   Jeffrey J. Selingo, "Why Are So Many College Students Failing to Gain Job Skills Before Graduation?," The Washington Post (WP Company, January 26, 2015), https://www.washingtonpost.com/news/grade-point/wp/2015/01/26/why-are-so-many-college-students-failing-to-gain-job-skills-before-graduation/.

7   "Graduates Lack Work-Ready Skills That Businesses Need During COVID Era," Bdaily Business News (Bdaily, March 17, 2021), https://bdaily.co.uk/articles/2021/03/17/graduates-lack-work-ready-skills-that-businesses-need-during-covid-era.

8   David M Walker, "More Companies Explore Hiring Independent Contractors Versus Employees," PRNewsWire, March 16, 2010, https://www.prnewswire.com/news-releases/more-companies-explore-hiring-independent-contractors-versus-employees-87804667.html.

9   Jessica Edgson, "27 Eye-Opening Outsourcing Statistics (April 2021 Update)," CapitalCounselor, April 2, 2021, https://capitalcounselor.com/outsourcing-statistics/.

10   Katherine Peralta, "Outsourcing to China Cost U.S. 3.2 Million Jobs Since 2001," USNews, December 11, 2014, https://www.usnews.com/news/blogs/data-mine/2014/12/11/outsourcing-to-china-cost-us-32-million-jobs-since-2001.

11   Andrew Bloomenthal, "Business Process Outsourcing (BPO)," Investopedia, December 27, 2020, https://www.investopedia.com/terms/b/business-process-outsourcing.asp.

12   William Pfeifer, "Learn About Legal Outsourcing," The Balance Small Business, January 28, 2020, https://www.thebalancesmb.com/outsourcing-legal-services-2151240.

13   Joe Konop, "How to Get Your Resume Read by an Employer," Forbes (Forbes Magazine, March 18, 2014), https://www.forbes.com/sites/nextavenue/2014/03/18/how-to-get-your-resume-read-by-an-employer/?sh=24db9a476865.

14   Danielle Elmers, "The Job-Search Statistics All Job Seekers Should Know," TopResume, October 15, 2021, https://www.topresume.com/career-advice/7-top-job-search-statistics.

15   Peter Economy, "11 Interesting Hiring Statistics You Should Know," Inc.com, May 5, 2015, https://www.inc.com/peter-economy/19-interesting-hiring-statistics-you-should-know.html.

16   Dr. John Sullivan, "Why You Can't Get A Job … Recruiting Explained By the Numbers," ERE Recruiting Intelligence, July 23, 2015, https://www.ere.net/why-you-cant-get-a-job-recruiting-explained-by-the-numbers/.

17   Chuck Palahniuk, *Fight Club: A Novel* (New York, NY: W.W. Norton & Company, 1996).

18   Christian Holub, "Chuck Palahniuk on Accidentally Inspiring the 'Snowflake' Insult," Entertainment Weekly, November 17, 2017, https://ew.com/books/2017/11/17/chuck-palahniuk-snowflake-insult/.

19   Shonna Waters, "Why You Need Executive Presence (And How to Get It)," BetterUp, June 8, 2021, https://www.betterup.com/blog/executive-presence.

20   Diana Tsai, "80% Of Jobs Are Not on Job Boards: Here's How to Find Them," Forbes (Forbes Magazine, October 2, 2017), https://www.forbes.com/sites/dianatsai/2017/10/02/80-of-jobs-are-not-on-job-boards-heres-how-to-find-them/?sh=5bff87d4551c.

21   Megan Bruneau, "5 Hacks for Overcoming Social Anxiety and Networking Like a Pro," Forbes (Forbes Magazine, May 28, 2016), https://www.forbes.com/sites/meganbruneau/2016/05/28/5-hacks-to-overcoming-social-anxiety-networking-like-a-pro/?sh=2aaa7ed9482b.

22   Kimberly Truong, "Can You Really Fake Confidence 'Til You Make It?," Refinery29, July 18, 2018, https://www.refinery29.com/en-us/faking-confidence-self-esteem#:~:text=Marni%20Amsellem%2C%20 PhD%2C%20a%20clinical,yourself%20and%20knowing%20your%20 worth.

23   Interview with Scott Johnson. Personal, November 4, 2021.

24   Interview with Alan Walker. Personal, November 10, 2021, and Interview with Scott Johnson. Personal, November 4, 2021.

25   Jack Kelly, "Harvard Business School Study Says Software Overlooks Millions Of Qualified Job Candidates: Here's How To Fight Back Against The Bots," Forbes (Forbes Magazine, September 7, 2021), https://www.forbes.com/sites/jackkelly/2021/09/07/harvard-business-school-study-says-software-overlooks-millions-of-qualified-job-candidates-heres-how-to-fight-back-against-the-bots/?sh=6735a22e1-3d3.

26   Interview with Alan Walker. Personal, November 10, 2021.

27   Interview with Scott Johnson. Personal, November 4, 2021.

28   Ibid.

29   Interview with Zach Frazier. Personal, October 13, 2021.

30   Chip Cutter, "People Are 'Ghosting' at Work, and It's Driving Companies Crazy," LinkedIn (LinkedIn, June 23, 2018), https://www.linkedin.com/pulse/people-ghosting-work-its-driving-companies-crazy-chip-cutter/.

31   Nick Morgan, "Why Do First Impressions Matter?," Forbes (Forbes Magazine, June 10, 2014), https://www.forbes.com/sites/nickmorgan/2014/06/10/why-do-first-impressions-matter/?sh=b750ac319ced.

32   "The Ultimate Guide to Building Confidence: Tony Robbins," tonyrobbins.com, accessed January 6, 2022, https://www.tonyrobbins. com/building-confidence/.

33   Asad Meah, "40 Inspirational Denis Waitley Quotes On Success," Awaken The Greatness Within, June 8, 2017, https://www. awakenthegreatnesswithin.com/40-inspirational-denis-waitley-quotes-on-success/.

34   Michele Debczak, "This Test Will Tell You How Many Books You Can Read in a Year," Mental Floss, January 17, 2019, https://www. mentalfloss.com/article/570929/how-many-books-to-read-year-test.

35   "Famous Failures: 23 Stories to Inspire You to Succeed," accessed January 12, 2022, https://www.bradaronson.com/famous-failures/.

36   Jocko Willink and Leif Babin, *Extreme Ownership: How U.S. Navy SEALs Lead and Win* (New York, NY: St. Martin's Press, 2015).

37   Leslie Ye, "The Psychology of Choice: How to Make Easier Decisions," HubSpot Blog, July 25, 2019, https://blog.hubspot.com/sales/the-psychology-of-choice.

38   Chip Cutter, "People Are 'Ghosting' at Work, and It's Driving Companies Crazy," LinkedIn (LinkedIn, June 23, 2018), https://www. linkedin.com/pulse/people-ghosting-work-its-driving-companies-crazy-chip-cutter/.

39   Interview with Sophie Theen. Personal, September 29, 2021.

40   Interview with Brad Johnson. Personal, September 3, 2021.

41   Interview with Sophie Theen. Personal, September 29, 2021.

42   "What Are Office Politics?," Corporate Finance Institute, November 8, 2020, https://corporatefinanceinstitute.com/resources/careers/soft-skills/office-politics/.

43   Interview with Alan Walker. Personal, November 10, 2021.

44   Marie Kondo and Scott Sonenshein, *Joy at Work* (New York, NY: Little, Brown Spark, 2020), 209.

45   Ibid, 214.

46   Vishnu Vardhan, "85% Of Job Success Comes from Having These Skills," LinkedIn, May 4, 2019, https://www.linkedin.com/pulse/85-job-success-comes-from-having-skills-vishnu-vardhan-/.

47   Justin Kerr, How to Be Great at Your Job: Get Things Done. Get
the Credit. Get Ahead. (San Francisco, CA: Chronicle Books, 2018), 58.

48   "Imply Definition & Meaning," Merriam-Webster, accessed January
6, 2022, https://www.merriam-webster.com/dictionary/imply.

49   "Infer Definition & Meaning," Merriam-Webster (Merriam-
Webster), accessed January 6, 2022, https://www.merriam-webster.com/
dictionary/infer.

50   Sander Flaum and Mechele Flaum, Boost Your Career: How to
Make an Impact, Get Recognized, and Build the Career You Want (New
York, NY: Allworth Press, 2017), 8-9.

51   Daniel Goleman, "What Makes a Leader?," Harvard Business
Review, January 2004, https://hbr.org/2004/01/what-makes-a-leader.

52   Steve Goldstein, "EQ Is Massively More Important Than IQ for
Leaders. Here's Why," Inc.com, September 26, 2017, https://www.inc.
com/steve-goldstein/eq-is-massively-more-important-than-iq-for-
leaders-heres-why.html.

53   Daniel Goleman, "What Makes a Leader?," Harvard Business
Review, January 2004, https://hbr.org/2004/01/what-makes-a-leader.

54   "Success Definition & Meaning," Merriam-Webster, accessed
January 6, 2022, https://www.merriam-webster.com/dictionary/success.

55   Interview with Mike Glass. Personal, September 15, 2021.

56   Mint, "How To Be a Career-Changing Mentor: 27 Tips To Make
a Difference," MintLife Blog, July 6, 2021, https://mint.intuit.com/blog/
early-career/how-to-be-a-mentor/.

57   Joanne Davila, "Stop Trying to Fix Things, Just Listen!," Psychology
Today, June 17, 2016, https://www.psychologytoday.com/us/blog/skills-
healthy-relationships/201606/stop-trying-fix-things-just-listen.

58   Pilita Clark, "Why Unlimited Holidays Mean More Time in the
Office," The Irish Times, November 5, 2017, https://www.irishtimes.
com/business/work/why-unlimited-holidays-mean-more-time-in-the-
office-1.3280668.

59   Jon Levy, "4 Ways Going on Vacation Increases Your Productivity,"
Inc.com (Inc., May 25, 2017), https://www.inc.com/jon-levy/4-science-
backed-reasons-vacations-increase-productivity.html.

60   Sherrie Bourg Carter, "The Tell Tale Signs of Burnout … Do You Have Them?," November 26, 2013, https://www.psychologytoday.com/us/blog/high-octane-women/201311/the-tell-tale-signs-burnout-do-you-have-them.

61   Alicia Nortje, "What Is Burnout? 16 Signs and Symptoms of Excessive Stress," Positive Psychology, December 14, 2021, https://positivepsychology.com/burnout/#physically-sick.

62   SWNS, "Most Americans Dream of Being Their Own Boss," New York Post, January 17, 2018, https://nypost.com/2018/01/17/most-americans-dream-of-being-their-own-boss/.

63   Chris Winfield, "7 Signs That You're Ready to Leave the 9-5 and Become Your Own Boss," Inc.com, February 28, 2017, https://www.inc.com/chris-winfield/7-signs-that-youre-ready-to-leave-the-9-5-and-become-your-own-boss.html.